What people are saying about …

SUDDENLY SINGLE

"With the help of the Wonderful Counselor, Kathey does an amazing job of helping those who find themselves suddenly single move from survival to revival and then to abundant life. This text is filled with questions and answers that need to be addressed by those in transition looking for transformation. Kathey provides words of compassion, wisdom, and encouragement that will minister to anyone in a season of singleness."

—**Dr. Sabrina Black**, international speaker,
president of National Biblical Counseling
Association, author of *Live Right Now*

"Having spent thousands of hours mediating divorce cases, I know Kathey Batey's *Suddenly Single* can help men and women as they face the process of being single.

—**Peter A. Letzmann**, court
mediator and attorney

"While divorce is a common occurrence in our society, the feelings it evokes are uncommonly intense. Insecurity, rejection, abandonment, anger, sadness, fear, and uncertainty to name a few. Kathey Batey's *Suddenly Single* is a welcome read for anyone who fits that description. This encouraging, enlightening book is written with gentle authority from one who's been there. I highly recommend it for anyone facing this major life transition.

—**C. Leslie Charles**, author of *Bless Your Stress* and *All Is Not Lost*

"Kathey Batey is the friend the newly single need so they can work through the pain and create a new life. Kathey has walked her talk. Her book is a wonderful blend of practical advice and powerful questions, exercises, and processes to get your life back on track. I just wish I knew Kathey and had her book when I became suddenly single! It would have saved me a lot of time and tears."

—**Judy Anderson**, Relating to Success coach and speaker

"Its time is now and its message is relevant and purposeful."

—**Dr. Jane Helmstead**, licensed professional counselor

"Accept *Suddenly Single* as a wonderful guidebook to help you navigate through the loneliness, anger, hurt, and confusion on your passage to reclaiming your life! Kathey doesn't shy away from addressing the tough issues singles face. She shares the message that life is not over when you find yourself suddenly single, you've begun a new life adventure you hadn't planned. I can't wait to put *Suddenly Single* into the hands of many of my coaching clients who desperately need it!"

—**Christine Schaap**, author of *Bring It On! Women Embracing Midlife*

"Based on my many years of working with newly single people, I've found *Suddenly Single* to be the best resource for people rebuilding their lives. Kathey Batey covers all the necessary topics of transition, healing, and the vital ingredients for starting a new life."

—Susan Zimmerman-President,
Passages Transition Center

"The best thing about *Suddenly Single* is that Kathey writes from her heart, and the genuineness of her journey is found on every page. She shares the depth of her pain, the rocky paths she traveled, and the profound life lessons she learned from her always-faithful God, who never let go and carried her through to the wisdom contained in these pages. This book can give you courage to face your pain, release the hurts, and find new freedom and joy for living your life!"

—Beth Bolthouse, licensed
professional counselor

"Not only does Kathey understand the pain, grief, and shame of divorce first-hand, she has also allowed God to use her experience to minister and bring comfort to others. As we were all reeling from the devastation of our circumstances, she would weekly encourage us declaring, 'It will get better.' She was so right! A year later, I am stronger and am living a more beautiful, fulfilled life than I could have ever imagined. Time is a great healer, and when we surrender to the process, God really can and does make all things new."

—Brenda, group participant

"The most beneficial for me were the questions that actually probed into the reality of being divorced, and trying to take positive steps forward and not remain stuck or depressed or overwhelmed by the emotional pain."

—**Don**, group participant

"What was most helpful was the emotional support. The positive attitude that even this will pass."

—**Isabel**, group participant

"This book made me think about things I wouldn't have otherwise thought about because I've been married for thirty-eight years (and I had to address certain issues)."

—**Janet**, group participant

"I have reread, underlined, and highlighted many things in my copy of *Suddenly Single*. It helped me survive the pain of divorce."

—**Jesse**, group participant

"Speaking and writing from experience, Kathey Batey writes and facilitates training as she guides you through the turbulent waters of finding yourself *Suddenly Single*. Kathey is a true leader in helping to ReDesign Your Life as you move forward."

—**Debra Carr**, founder of Image for MEN

SUDDENLY SiNGLE

REBUILDING YOUR LIFE AFTER DIVORCE

KATHEY BATEY

DAVID C COOK

transforming lives together

SUDDENLY SINGLE
Published by David C Cook
4050 Lee Vance Drive
Colorado Springs, CO 80918 U.S.A.

David C Cook U.K., Kingsway Communications
Eastbourne, East Sussex BN23 6NT, England

The graphic circle C logo is a registered trademark of David C Cook.

Details in some stories have been changed to protect
the identities of the persons involved.

LCCN 2017949833
ISBN 978-1-4347-1172-4
eISBN 978-0-8307-7216-2

The Team: Alice Crider, Margot Starbuck, Amy Konyndyk,
Diane Gardner, Rachael Stevenson, Susan Murdock
Cover Design: Nick Lee
Cover Photo: Getty Images

Printed in the United States of America
First Edition 2018

1 2 3 4 5 6 7 8 9 10

012818

This book is dedicated to you, who have found yourself suddenly single and to all the potential in your future, whether you can see it right now or not.

And this book is dedicated to the God of second chances, who believes in us more than we believe in ourselves.

Do not call to mind the former things, or ponder things of the past. Behold, I will do something new, now it will spring forth; will you not be aware of it? I will even make a roadway in the wilderness, rivers in the desert.

Isaiah 43:18–19 NASB

CONTENTS

DEAR READER

I see you, I know where you are, and I know where you've been. I was there once, twenty-one years ago, when I went through my own divorce. Hang on. There is hope. I found it; I've seen it; I know it. You can know it too.

For the past twelve years, I have worked, both one-on-one and in groups, with hundreds of people going through divorce. I've seen people survive, gain incredible strength, and surprise themselves. I have worked with adults of every age and every socioeconomic class. Many times I've watched them remarry, but sometimes they remain happily single. Either way, there is hope you will grow beyond this life transition and make it a place to launch from. Your story doesn't end here.

On the day my marriage ended—then again one week later, and even months later—I was an emotional, physical, and financial mess. I felt disoriented, confused, traumatized, and distraught. But I still had to function daily and manage life and kids, just like you do. This is where I learned to trust the healing process and move through it intentionally. Yes, there is a process to healing. That process takes you from the emotions of grief, anger, and loneliness to acceptance and the strength and confidence to move forward. There are stages to work through that enable you to journey past this. This process is not as fast as you want it to be, but if you are patient in working through it the process will make you a stronger person.

Wherever you are today in this journey, you will survive and grow beyond the current turmoil. How do I know this? Because you were brave enough to pick up this book and begin to read it. And as you continue through it, you will find the pieces of a broken-life puzzle and you will put your life back together again, even better and stronger. This is a painful, yet powerful time. Trusting the process begins now. This trek requires the honesty to grieve and to grow, faith to believe, and a willingness to celebrate the steps forward and successes along the way.

This book extends my compassion to you. More importantly it provides a catalyst for you to incorporate God's love and healing into your life. God will prove Himself real and practical if you search for Him during this time. Your rawness gives you a sensitivity that can be used to find God. Don't waste this painful, yet powerful time. It will restructure, reorganize, and reestablish your life forever. Read this book with pen in hand. Write on its pages; cry over its words. The pain you are experiencing is real and devastating and damaging. But how much it damages you will depend on if you leverage this time for your growth and benefit.

Before you begin this book, I want to acknowledge and honor marriage as a holy communion. I do not intend to dishonor marriage or encourage divorce. I hate divorce, and I understand why God hates it. It damages people, especially children. But when it happens, people need support and guidance. This book gives those who are going through divorce tools and techniques to better understand themselves and the process they are going through at this critical time of transition.

Please note: there is no Prince (or Princess) Charming at the end of this book; the next relationship is not the answer to your life right now. Heal and gain strength before you consider a new relationship. Jumping in too early complicates your life before you are ready to handle it. Use this transition time to heal, rediscover who you are, and determine your purpose. God has great things for you. Prepare yourself for them.

This book's goal is to help you create a full and purposeful life in the wake of your divorce, whether you were the one who left or the one who was left. If you've been traveling the divorce journey for a while, you'll find the principles in this book true, and they will hopefully reaffirm your own truths and help you encounter perspectives through which you can learn more from your own story.

You might begin this experience focused on your loss, but my intention is that you will finish this book ready to create a new, fulfilling life.

1

MY STORY KNOWS YOUR STORY

Sometimes God lets you hit rock bottom so that you
will discover He is the Rock at the bottom.

Tony Evans

Jonathon never was a morning person, but mornings early in his divorce were the worst. He couldn't sleep most nights, until he finally drifted off just in time for the alarm to buzz and remind him where he left off, in this painful crisis. His body felt like a ton of bricks, the weight of emotional pain, suffocating. His bewilderment acted as a heavy drug, diminishing his concentration and good decision-making. Emotions overruled everything for a time. A company executive, he found hiding his anguish from others challenging. His kids were bewildered too. They went through rituals like robots. Joy had been sucked out of the house like a vacuum. Any sense of peace was elusive.

I've heard the sleepless night stories many times. Emotions are killers in the early stages of divorce. Does this sound familiar to you?

YOUR UNIQUE STORY

Though you have your own unique story of divorce, parts of your story may be like Jonathan's or mine. It's a bond none of us wanted or pursued. But here we are, relating in our confusion and pain. The beautiful thing about life is that change can bring good. And the rest of your story isn't written yet. God gives you the pen to write the ending.

You may be new to the divorce process and at the beginning stage of shock and emotion. I promise you won't stay there.

Your reactions, strange thoughts, and uncharacteristic behaviors are natural and normal for what you are going through. It is your pain working itself out.

Your story brings you to this disorienting time where life hurls out of control. It is a bizarre and confusing place, and you're probably feeling very alone. I understand, and I'm here to walk this road with you. More importantly, I hope you'll sense God's presence along the way.

Our stories begin with shock, pain, guilt, and shame, then progress to acceptance, understanding, and growth. Although you start your story in grief and pain, you can finish healed, purposeful, and ready to make the best of your story. Trust me: even though you don't feel it now, it will happen.

Besides divorce, you and I have another bond. It's called hope and life after divorce. And if you can't see it in your current sorrow and despair, I understand.

As I share my story, it may resonate with yours. It may have similar pains, disappointments, and heartaches. I am in the trenches with you, and I know what you are experiencing.

MY STORY

For me, becoming suddenly single began when my husband announced he was leaving. It was his conclusion to our bad marriage. The shock and pain I experienced defies words. Along with the feelings of physical, emotional, and spiritual betrayal, I felt as if someone had destroyed my life's work. We had been married for twenty years and were raising three great children, then in their teens. The pain and injustice was both to our children and to me. His choice to leave our home and our family sent me reeling. Gone was the security of family support. Gone were the family goals, dinners, discussions, vacations, and memories. Gone was the camping, dreaming, plotting, scheming, retiring, or deciding who would mow the lawn. Gone was the truck pulling into the driveway, his opening of the front door, and his going out of the same. Gone were the things we had worked twenty years for. I could not help but feel they were snatched out from underneath me.

Our marriage didn't dissolve overnight. Over the years, our relationship had become a business relationship instead of a marriage. We grew apart, living independent of each other, not tending to or honoring each other. He had worked years building a business; I was overseeing the lives of three teenagers, working full time, and handling all the details of a busy time of life. Were we so busy, preoccupied, because the relationship lacked. Or did the relationship lack because we were preoccupied? Whichever came first, the relationship withered and died. The times we truly connected were rare. I now see the emptiness of our relationship. Like many of the couples I have seen, we went on for years, living together while leading separate lives.

Many times throughout the marriage I thought, *If I just work harder, if I'm good enough, surely things will work out. Keep pursuing, keep going, keep pretending.* Yet we woke up one morning and found our marriage dead. I'm just not sure which morning it was.

As empty as it became, some good things came from our marriage. We were blessed with three beautiful children: two daughters and one son. Had this marriage never happened, I would be without them, and my heart pains at that thought. There were fabulous moments to appreciate in my marriage.

Like me, did you hope your spouse would one day wake up and realize all you had been blessed with and built together? Sadly, many times people don't see those blessings because unspoken expectations cloud their perception.

UNSPOKEN EXPECTATIONS

With the benefit of hindsight, I see how unspoken expectations can damage a marriage. We all have ideas of how a marriage relationship should be. Influenced by the families we came from, societal norms, cultural dictates, peer pressure, and more, all of us carry specific expectations, and live and wait for the fulfillment of what we expect of a spouse. Sometimes, we don't articulate or explain them to each other; we just expect them. We have frameworks about things such as men's roles, women's roles, how pot roast is made, and how a couple earns an income. We have expectations of emotional support, or that certain character traits are valued. And then we struggle to make life live up to these expectations.

In my marriage, our unexpressed expectations made it difficult to reach each other. They created a wall between us we could neither see nor get past, and though we denied or failed to acknowledge their existence, our expectations were real, and far more influential than we realized.

We dealt with conflict in unhealthy ways; we stuffed our frustration and hurts. We expected the other person to mind read and understand our feelings, and we failed to hear what was not being said. When feelings were expressed, they were not valued. I shut down emotionally early in the marriage, and somewhere along the way he did too. I shut down because my vital needs were unmet—I longed for emotional support; for encouragement as a person with gifts, dreams, and talents; and to be cherished and recognized as an individual as well as a wife and mother. My expectations to have those needs met shut down too. I turned elsewhere—into my children's lives and to writing plays for church. Inside I felt incredibly lonely and misunderstood.

My husband and I were isolated people living in the same house. We were both left lonely and wanting for intimate connection. Our dysfunctional cycle continued for years. This is not unique to us. Do you see any similarities in your life?

Denial of problems and incompatibility can hide issues for a while, even years if you work hard enough at it. But the truth always, eventually shows up, blatantly glaring and undeniable any longer. After my husband slept on the couch every night for a year, he took action to get out of the marriage. I suppose it seems odd I was shocked, but I was. For many years, I denied the distance between us. But deep inside I knew I had lost respect for this man and he had no love left for me. The hurt was incredible. But facing the painful and ugly truth actually brought relief. The truth, while difficult to accept, is easier to deal with than continuing to deny what is real. At least you know what you are now living *is* real.

SINGLE THOUGHTS

- What unexpressed expectations existed in your relationship?
- In what areas was there denial, for yourself and for your partner?
- What painful truth gives clarity to you so you can begin to grieve this relationship?

HITTING BOTTOM

I thought I'd hit bottom the day the divorce papers came. The door, through which my husband had always come home to us now closed behind him for the last time. I stood alone in our empty house.

The moment of our lowest point will differ for each of us, but it does come in divorce. It hits hard with feelings of abandonment, isolation, and pain. The bottom is a dark and dreary place, and you feel like you're suffocating. You force yourself to breathe and move through it one moment at a time.

But then your husband comes back for his things and the bottom plunges deeper. He talks about dividing your life into two separate piles. This person you once lived in intimacy with is now a stranger, a distant adversary. The lawyer calls to discuss details, and this outsider takes your spouse's place to discuss your future. How odd. How strange. How wrong.

Divorce is a death in many ways. It is the death of a marriage. You have to go through a grieving process and adjust your mind that the relationship has died even while you see the other person as a ghost, walking around haunting you.

I cried.

You cry and you hurt. Words, thoughts, and feelings bounce off and inside of you at the same time. You are confused, disoriented, physically drained. Churning with feelings of guilt, shame, betrayal, rejection, abandonment, deception, inadequacy, isolation, and loss, you grieve deeply.

If you left your mate, you also feel confused, disoriented, and physically drained. You likely feel the full gamut of guilt, shame, betrayal, rejection, abandonment, inadequacy, isolation, loss, and grief. And it is important to note, if you are not currently experiencing these things, you may have processed a lot of this emotion and despair prior to leaving the marriage.

Even if you and your spouse mutually decided to end the marriage, you do not escape these feelings. The pain remains as prominent in you as in anyone. You feel like a failure at one of the most important commitments you have ever made and a disappointment to many. It takes time to heal this gaping wound.

Faults are found at the end of every broken marriage. Sometimes it is the cheating, lying, gambling, drinking, affairs, and differing lifestyle changes; there is no pain-free divorce when two imperfect people are involved. Fault finding is just a way to try to make sense of what is happening to you. It's natural, but not helpful and may cost you more energy than you have to spare right now.

If you feel as if you are at the bottom right now, don't despair. This is part of your transitional process and part of the passage. This portion of your journey is a dark, dreary tunnel, but there is another side—your future, not too far in the distance. I assure you it's there.

Hope will come; healing will happen. Time and wise counsel will help heal your shattered heart. Your future will offer possibilities that have never crossed your mind before, because you were not in a place where they could. Wrap your arms around your own soul and hold on. Ease your hurt by accepting support and offers of help from those who care about you. This is not a process you can rush through.

MOVING BEYOND DESPAIR

Mercifully, during this darkness, light pierces through. There is the light of wise counsel from a pastor or friend and the light of truly understanding how Christ suffers with you in these personal moments. The light when you have a need met unexpectedly and you realize you are not alone or the light of kindness from a friend's warm touch. In the middle of all the chaos and confusion dwells the spirit of survival. I had it, and I pray you have it too. I was not completely abandoned. My spirit had a Comforter who gave me a sense of support I had never experienced before. Of course, I had never been in this place before. This tiny pinprick of light, that sense of knowing there was something beyond despair, was hope. No matter how dark it seems at any moment, look for the small glimmers of hope and light to hold on to. They will help you crawl up from the bottom toward life.

For me, the brightest light was my faith, the source of hope I had built years before. The foundation of my faith had supported me in the past, and it was strong enough to hold me now. Somehow I knew, even through it all, God was there.

Faith is believing something awaits beyond this dark time and that God, in His economy, uses all our life experiences for our growth. This faith allows you to survive the pain, injustice, fear, and despair. It is the core belief that no matter what happens, God is with you and for you. This faith keeps you from being overwhelmed by negative emotions and self-doubt. Even the smallest bit of faith can secure you when you hold on to it. Make your faith stubborn and refuse to give up. Search to find God in all this mess. He is there.

Anchor yourself within your faith, because your emotions will run the gamut. There will be occasions when you think you're going to make it, and then the next minute there will be despair. You will have times of confidence and times of fear. You will have moments of insight and acceptance and then crash into moments of anger. Your heart will feel as if every touch of human kindness is like a cooling stroke to burning flesh. Your brain will feel numb, yet it will be sensitive to every note of a soulful song you hear.

I know where you are, but the beautiful truth is you are not going to stay there. Your story is not finished. This is a sacred season to heal. Give it the respect it deserves, because this portion of your life is not wasted. This season matters.

2

THIS SEASON MATTERS

*It is in the middle of misery that so much becomes clear. The
one who says nothing good comes of this is not yet listening.*

Clarissa Pinkola Estes

Marcy went through her divorce in so much pain that she barely
spoke a word when she came into the divorce support group. A
victim of domestic abuse, she had lived a facade while married to a
prestigious man in the community. She had a lot to hide, and she hid
it well. She also had several children who had witnessed this abuse
and experienced their own. After her husband pushed her through a
glass door, Marcy had enough. She filed for divorce, moved out, and
took her children with her.

As the weeks went on, Marcy grew stronger in her tone and
attitude. She found a modest apartment and peace, which she
hadn't experienced in a very long time. She took control of her
life. It felt more real and honest than ever before. She learned to
care for herself in a healthy way and to understand how God views
submission in marriage. She realized God loved her enough to
grant her safety and grace to leave the marriage. Her husband in

his abuse had stopped loving her as Christ loved the church. Her struggles weren't solved overnight, but with wise decisions, Marcy made her life work out beautifully. I've watched her progress over several years, and her countenance says it all. I've met many women (and men) who left an abusive relationship when the marriage covenant was abandoned to violence. Ironically, some feel extreme guilt for taking a stand to survive. God never desires a person to be mistreated and dishonored in a marriage relationship. A person is more important than a marriage. Marriage is a license to love and protect, not to control and harm. When Marcy embraced this truth, she used this transitional time to build a healthy and safe life for herself and her children. She found this time had greater value than she ever expected.

The transition into the single life is a strange time, and a powerful one. In fact, I am convinced it is one of life's most transformative experiences because of your sensitivity in it. Your transition can be perilous or productive, rich with lessons and insights or ignored to your detriment. It will be the most powerful when you work on healing instead of jumping into your next relationship. Pay attention to the experiences you are going through and learn from them. Take advantage of opportunities that can help stabilize you by seeking help or counseling, talking with close friends, or journaling your thoughts and struggles.

Take good care of yourself during this time. Be aware of the choices you make and the people you let into your life and heart. Guard against negative thinking, such as *I don't care anymore*, or *Nothing matters now*. Rationalizing and justifying self-defeating behaviors is normal when you are going through a crisis and are facing depression caused by divorce. Understand this is part of the territory and this too shall pass. You matter greatly. This is not your final destination; this is a passage. You can leverage this passage and decide to navigate its waters into a powerful life. The fog will clear and the hurt will lessen. You can and will feel whole again.

HOW WE FEEL ABOUT OURSELVES IN DIVORCE

After working with hundreds of people going through divorce, I do not recall ever finding one who felt good about him- or herself while going through this crisis. Unless one is totally narcissistic and unable to comprehend what is happening, everyone feels insecure, rejected, and inadequate. It is the normal way to feel during this process.

As you journey through this trauma, your soul may feel deeply wounded. Your value as a human being has been assaulted. Your appearance, mind, mental capabilities, decisions, sexuality, parenting, status, and relation to the world may all come under judgment and into question. Surely you can relate to one or two of these; you may even relate to all of them. As a result, you may find yourself in a very dark place where you question if you should be living at all. (As if only perfect people should be allowed to live and function in life.) If these are your thoughts, reach out and seek help. This is tough stuff to deal with and hard work that can be overwhelming at times. The only way through it *is through it*, one day at a time.

Please understand your view of yourself and your life in general is distorted during this time. You may be tempted to make some conclusions about yourself and life right now. Please don't. You cannot see things realistically at the moment. There may be things to sort out in your life, but during the divorce is not the ideal time to address them. Hold off. That is for another transition stage that we will discuss later, but for now go easy on yourself! This is the time for self-care and healing.

You are under a lot of stress during divorce, which can make you feel inadequate to handle it all. As much as we wish the world would stop and let us off for a while, it keeps moving. So be compassionate with yourself and take life an hour or a day at a time. If you are moving, albeit slowly, you are still progressing. This is not a race. Do not expect to climb mountains; congratulate yourself for managing small bumps in the road.

The world can seem crushing at this point. Hold on to a truth about yourself: you are loved by an infinite God; He will sustain you. Remember battles you've conquered in the past, successes you've had, and lean on God's strength to get you through this one. Even if God has been a stranger until now, sit in His presence. Let His Spirit love you. Listen to the quiet and know God wants to draw near to you and comfort you. Read Psalm 139 and consider how God thinks about you. Look at those words and focus on them instead of the negative ones you may be hearing.

Words are powerful, and we struggle with our self-concept due to the words that have been spoken against us. Hurtful words, whether they came from you or from your spouse, are damaging.

Words spoken aloud or implied through actions, such as attitudes of disgust, condescension, or rejection, can make us believe lies about ourselves for years, especially if we've heard and seen them for years. The lies you might hear directly or subtly are: "You are not good enough, pretty enough, handsome enough, smart enough, or sophisticated enough." When lies like these repeat in your mind, whisper Jesus's name and ask Him to help you know the truth. Feed His truth to the lies when they surface. There is power in God's Word. Learn it and say it. Stand in His goodness, His "enoughness." And move forward toward a life rich in purpose and power because of this truth. You are enough just as you are right now. If you have never accepted this truth, now is your time. You don't have to go through this alone.

Find a safe place for your words to and about yourself in a friend, counselor, or support group that will listen to you. Watch your words during this time (especially in front of the children). Make them as optimistic as possible and do not let words others may fling at you penetrate your heart. Your former spouse or others may speak out of their pain too. Understanding when pain is speaking may help you see yourself and them more objectively instead of accepting false words as the truth.

Give up unrealistic expectations of yourself during this time. This is not the time to be a tough soldier; it is a time to care for yourself and seek help when necessary. Now is the moment to back off from life's business and tend to the business of you. Care for yourself by finding someone to confide in; seek counseling or a support group. Care for your body, your emotions, and your mind, and guard what you allow into it. Maybe it is time to step back from your schedule and allow others to take the lead.

After the divorce, in your healing you will begin to learn positive truths about yourself. God can redeem your thoughts through Jesus Christ. Perspectives will change, and you will gain insight on your marriage and yourself that will help you grow into a stronger, better person. Just make it through the days in the early stages of divorce. That is enough accomplishment!

JUST PLAIN MESSY

On the day my divorce was supposed to finalize, my husband called. He said instead of pursuing this divorce and going through with it, he desired reconciliation. He wanted our family back together again. I embraced the move, and I embraced him.

He came back to the same world he left. We still lacked the ability to communicate or fix what was wrong with our marriage. The wall of expectations stood impenetrable between us. The marriage counselor was right when he told us we were in counseling ten years too late. Five days after my husband came back, he left again. The low point I reached the second time was deeper than the first. It was darker, colder, and more isolated than before. Maybe because this time it was hopeless, and I knew it really was the end. I had given my marriage one more chance, only to see it fail again. I gave it one more chance because so much was at stake—my precious family and the rest of my life.

Standing in the kitchen feeling helpless, I asked God to hold me. "Please, just hold me," was all I could utter. In the quiet of that afternoon, He did. I found His presence at that particular time of need. I discovered a fullness of faith and a knowledge that in the kitchen, I was not alone. And He hasn't left me since.

As you search for strength and comfort, whether you find yourself at the bottom for the first or second time, you can discover what you need to make it through. At that moment, God will hold you. Accept this; it will bring you hope to begin healing.

Giving my marriage the final effort and another chance actually allowed me to have closure. I knew I had put forth the final attempt to save my marriage. This gave me strength, and when the offer came again for reconciliation, I had the stamina to say no. I had given my marriage the honor it deserved, the final chance to make things work. This was a turning point for me. I gained power and dignity by setting boundaries that valued my own soul and by refusing to be yo-yoed any further. I determined how I would be treated, which helped me find closure and protection for myself against further abuse and hurt.

Only you can decide when you know you are finished and there is no more discussion. But when you do, you will find a much-needed peace during this tumultuous time.

BOUNDARIES OF PROTECTION

I understood the offense to my soul was a spiritual issue. By setting mental and spiritual boundaries, I determined once and for all what was acceptable, whom I would open myself up to, and whom I would trust. My confidants, both family and friends, had totally changed since the divorce. The same will be true for you: not everyone is good or safe for you right now.

The man who was once my husband became an unsafe person for me, because at this point in my life he did not love me or care for my future. That meant I could no longer trust him or take any of his words or actions at face value. His decisions and opinions could no longer influence my life. With prayers for discernment and strength

I would now make my own decisions about what would work for me and my children.

Understanding your spouse is unsafe is a shift that takes a while to comprehend and adopt. And as much as your heart wants to go back to the routine of comfort and trust you've had in the past, it could be to your detriment.

Setting boundaries was a huge step for me. The decision to say no to further conversation, arguments, or explanations of myself to him gave me strength to continue, the power to move forward, and the ability to find my way out of the darkness of divorce. This turning point did not end the turmoil, but it ended my confusion. By establishing healthy boundaries, I gained respect and the courage to stand up for myself. My former husband couldn't just show up when he wanted; he couldn't assume how I thought or what I would allow. He had to ask about and wait for my decisions. I didn't allow myself to focus on rejection and all the second-guessing that comes with it. *Why wasn't I worth fighting for? Why was I so unlovable to him now? What is the matter with me?* God's hope, love, and comfort replaced those spiritual lies.

Recovering from divorce means facing a time of challenge, defining your value, and reestablishing who you are. Give yourself respect, structure, and protection by setting your boundaries, mind-set, and message: "I will not engage in conversation or actions in which I am treated poorly. I will respect and value myself. I will take power over my own life." See your value and take a stand for it. Recognize what is harmful or negative to you and do not allow it into your life. You have a voice, door, and disconnect button if necessary.

Also realize you have the right *not* to respond, discuss, or argue details. Don't allow yourself to be dragged into arguing and fighting.

In your past you may have felt obligated to respond to every question and to be accountable for your actions and for the details of your choices. But life's rules have just changed. You don't have to figure everything out, other than what directly affects you and your children, if you have children. This is for your protection, and the children's protection too. It is important to know when to hold on to hope for this relationship, but it is equally important to know when to shut off unproductive discussion.

Julie decided it was in her best interest to only communicate facts to her husband. No extra conversation about feelings, thoughts, or attitudes. Since she and her husband were unable to be civil to each other, this served them both well. They would text essential information about the children. It was not ideal, but it was better than conflict in front of the children.

How do you determine your boundaries and a healthy mind-set? Start by refusing to be the victim of your situation. Then keep your emotions in check. Do not let your feelings overwhelm, paralyze, or control you. Stand your ground for what is right for you and the children. And then only grant safe people access to your life and heart. Simplify your life as much as possible and decide to go beyond the injustice or bitterness, because dwelling on negatives renders you powerless.

I know your story of abuse, neglect, betrayal, injustice, and disrespect. I've heard it many times. There is no benefit for you in being the victim. You must find a place to launch from this. If you choose to be the victim, you will remain the victim. Even our mighty Savior wants you to seek, ask, knock, and pray—to learn to stand, even if on shaky legs. He will always be there to hold you up.

Waiting on the Lord is an *active* motion toward moving forward. We pray in silence to hear His direction, to hear His comfort and hope, and to gain motivation. But we act in inner strength to stand for our future and ourselves.

Some individuals live with the proverbial sword piercing their hearts for years, even a lifetime, and never get past the trauma of divorce. They show and tell their wounds over and over again. People can get stuck in the injustice and make it part of their identity instead of taking steps toward healing. You must launch from that place of pain, but you don't have to do it alone. Christ will be there. Come up from the bottom to explore what is now possible in your life that wasn't before. Embrace the words of author Christine Mason Miller: "At any given moment, you have the power to say: This is not how the story is going to end."[1]

SINGLE THOUGHTS

- What boundaries did you have in your past relationship?
- What boundaries have you set for yourself now?
- What is your mind-set at this moment? Do you see hope and possibility? Why or why not?

FINDING HOPE

Hope comes to us in different forms. Watch for it in surprising places, and when it comes, hold on to it with fervency. In one of my moments of despair, my wise and beautiful friend Dorothy looked me in the eye with hopeful determination and said, "Kathey, you're going to be all right." It sounds so simple, but to me at that time, her reassurance was profound. Her words brought hope to my dismal, hurting heart.

A wonderful, retired pastor once asked, "How can I pray for you?" I'll always remember how that question made me feel. He gave me no words of advice, no judgment, just understanding and love I needed so much. It is like the Jesus I know: "The LORD is near to the brokenhearted and saves those who are crushed in spirit" (Ps. 34:18 NASB). Listen to the tender, giving words people extend to you—savor them, accept them, and don't let them pass by unnoticed. Let your mind wrap around them and allow them to minister to you.

In the middle of your struggles and pain you will experience moments of love and caring that will give you hope and reprieve to your aching heart. God bless the people who are compassionate enough to care for you in times of tragedy. You will be surprised by those who show up to care for you and also surprised by those who disappear during this time, people you thought would be there. Don't despair; best friends, couple friends, and close family appear or disappear during this time and reveal a lot to you about loyalty, kindness, and integrity.

Who are those people who have been there for you? Focus on them. Keep your eyes open for people who cross your path and give you what you need. Receive their words of encouragement, kind deeds, and compassionate touch. This may be the first time you have ever had to reach out in need. You must allow yourself to do so. Receiving help, support, and comfort from others may feel awkward, but it's necessary. You will remember this in the future when others who are hurting reach out to you.

RECEIVING SUPPORT

Divorce may be the deepest hurt of your lifetime. You have permission to grieve. This is difficult stuff. While facilitating divorce groups over the years, I have witnessed many moments of pain. The hurt is real.

At age sixty-three, Lucy had to start her life over when her husband of thirty-three years not only left her but gambled away all of their retirement savings. She never knew he was gambling beyond his weekly lottery ticket. Jack joined the group after his wife left him while he was fighting cancer. Angela discovered she had an STD during an annual checkup, which revealed her husband's affairs on business trips while she was home raising their children. I've met pastors who left the church because they had an affair, or because their spouses did, and it destroyed their ministry. Many couples stopped communicating a long time ago; they were already divorced, just living in the same house. The heartbreak of divorce merits a time of grief.

Which of the above stories can you relate to? Allow your feelings to be honest, real, and raw. It's okay. In fact, it is necessary. I've seen men and women, from CEOs to stay-at-home moms, break down and sob like little children. Give yourself permission to feel how you feel. Let yourself grieve this huge loss. You need other people right now. You need to express your pain and to reach out and know you are not alone at this critical time. It's difficult to be vulnerable, yet it helps us recover. Needing help and being vulnerable is a universal condition we all will find ourselves in at one time or another. Divorce is a great leveler of humanity.

Although divorce has become common in our society, for those involved it is a huge loss. The ripping of flesh illustrates it best. In marriage we become one flesh, emotionally, spiritually, and financially. When we divorce the tear goes deep and everyone is affected—children, friends, and extended family. Your community is emotionally wounded, and the family tree will never be the same.

Please understand that family and friends are also processing your divorce. And many times, because they don't know what to say, they say nothing. Though understandable, this can make you feel even more isolated. We all perceive loss and change differently, and some simply don't know how to react. If they wish to withdraw or remain silent, let them be. Chances are they would like to help, but don't know how. Save your energy for recovery for yourself and your kids.

SINGLE THOUGHTS

- Who has supported you through this time? Right now, make a list of the people who are there for you. Then ask yourself whom you could reach out to for the help you need.
- Who has disappointed you?
- Who has exceeded your expectations?

RECLAIMING YOUR FUTURE

Like a car on a frightening roller coaster, my emotions in those early days were often shaky, scary, and unpredictable. I found myself holding my breath and then praying for encouragement to move forward. I lived moment by moment, reminding myself to breathe and hold on, to know this out-of-control ride would eventually come to a stop. My biggest fear each day was that I would start asking myself the questions that would launch the frightening ride again: *How did our marriage come to this? Can I make it on my own? What will happen to me now? What's on the other side of divorce? Do I have the strength to make it through this and make it on my own?*

Living one day at a time may sound simplistic, but it works. In the depth of my pain, I could not look too far into my future—I'd feel overwhelmed, paralyzed, and terrified. Sometimes to survive I could only focus on one hour at a time. I had to talk myself through the hours and ask myself simple questions:

- *Can I get out of bed this morning?*
- *Do I need to take the day off, or can I function enough to get through today?*
- *Can I muster up the energy to take a shower?*
- *Can I get the kids off to school, give them their lunch money, and remind them of their ride arrangements for sports?*
- *Do I need to sit down and give myself permission to cry?*

The frightening roller coaster ride does eventually end. It is not a sudden stop or an early one, but I promise you this disorientation does indeed end. For your sanity right now, slow down and focus on each moment, each day at a time.

SINGLE THOUGHTS

- What is your biggest fear right now?
- Where do you find strength to get through the day?
- What is the best thing you are doing for yourself to help you persevere through this time?

YOUR STORY IS UNIQUE

Every divorce story is unique. I shared a part of mine hoping you will see I understand what you are going through. If a feeling of betrayal is your number one emotion, I understand that emotion. I have known the drama, the abandonment, the betrayal of an affair, and the humiliating stories and phone calls that followed. Whatever your story, I understand what you are going through. I understand the confusion and pain. Whether you were the one to leave or you were left behind, you hurt in many of the same ways.

You will spend time in this turmoil, and then there will be a turning point. The rest of this book will be tools and help to get through the turmoil, the transition, and begin building your future. I'll walk with you through the process of becoming a strong and healthy single person, standing strong on your own, and living again. If you let Him, God will be there: "When you pass through deep waters, I will be with you; your troubles will not overwhelm you. When you pass through fire, you will not be burned; the hard trials that come will not hurt you" (Isa. 43:2 GNT).

In the coming chapters we will look at finding wise counsel, making good decisions, starting over, taking risks (and even enjoying them), nurturing existing relationships, and beginning new ones. Becoming suddenly single can be miserable or it can be a pathway toward a beautiful life. The first important step is allowing yourself the time to grieve so you can begin to heal.

3

GRIEVING AND HEALING

Grief does not change you.... It reveals you.

John Green

I was deep in the usual low "hum of numb" as I strolled through the backyard of my eight-acre property one summer evening at dusk. (The "hum of numb" is what I call the surreal, disoriented state you find yourself in when you go through the trauma of divorce. You are functioning in survival mode. Every sound and movement in your life comes with this reverberating hum of pain, disorientation, and imbalance.) The walk to the pond where I went to clear my head from the many issues facing this life transition was short. I watched the ripples in the water as fish came up to the dock waiting for food. I wandered on and brushed past the fruit-bearing branches of the apple tree in the backyard.

Being numb was the norm in the days after the divorce. My husband had moved out. The marital home would soon be mine alone. I wanted it for the children's stability and for me. I loved the country setting, the woods teeming with trillium, jack-in-the pulpit, streams, and wildlife. I knew the minute I walked through the door of the house eight years earlier that it was home. It felt, smelled, and looked like home to me. My soul lived there. The deep pond harbored bass, perch, and a few catfish; it was where the kids fished, swam, and boated. The backyard offered a park setting; the large lawn hosted many youth groups, family reunions, gatherings, and parties. Being a country girl, I found the four hours on the tractor to mow the grass a time of escape into mindless thought and a nice break from my day job and raising three teenagers who were busy with sports, homework, and friends.

That evening as the night sky darkened, I approached the south side of the house beside the barn. I heard a thump in front of the house. It was an odd sound, and I moved to the front yard to see what it was.

As I walked farther to the driveway I spotted our Rottweiler, Sadie, lying in the middle of the road. Panicking, I ran into the street to retrieve her. She wasn't dead, but she wasn't moving. I shouted to the cars, which came at me with their headlights on. I approached Sadie, then dragged her off the road. Fortunately, the oncoming cars avoided hitting me.

I brought her onto the grass then ran into the house to my youngest daughter, Melanie. I told her I was running Sadie to the vet clinic immediately. She helped me lift our ninety-pound pup into the car and sat in the back with Sadie while I drove. I stretched my right arm back to touch Sadie, praising her all the way on what a good girl she was.

By the time we arrived at the clinic, Sadie was bleeding from her eyes. The vet gently informed us that any chance of her survival would require traveling to the university veterinary hospital, three hours away. There was neither time nor money for that. Sadie was dying.

I stayed with her while they administered the final euthanasia shot. I stroked her and told her again and again, "You are a good girl Sadie, Mama's good girl" until she stilled. The staff helped us load her in the car for a quiet, dark drive home. The low hum of numb held a deeper drone of sadness.

When we turned into the driveway, we glimpsed the back of a small gray animal about ten yards ahead on the road. "We need to tell the neighbor about her cat," said Melanie. The knowledge that he too was killed earlier saddened us.

As I entered the house, I called for our small dog, Cricket. With the loss of our best dog ever, Sadie, whom we'd had for four years, I needed the consolation of Cricket who had been our family dog for twelve years—our first family dog all the kids grew up with. As I called out, there was no response. No usual running up to meet me with tail wagging and obnoxious jumping on my leg in a plea to be held and praised. The quiet stunned me. "Oh God, no, please." I ran outside, and there in the middle of the road lay Cricket. He'd been there the whole time we were gone. It wasn't the neighbor's cat; it was Cricket in the road. I was so consumed with Sadie, I hadn't given Cricket a thought until now.

The dogs were family members. They were in the family pictures, they were a part of Christmas gift-giving, and they slept with us. I cried harder for those dogs than I ever have cried in my life. They were more than animals. They symbolized our family. And if somehow the reality of the divorce and the end of a beautiful family unit had not been realized fully, the death of those dogs made it painfully clear.

The kids and I buried the dogs under the apple tree, and my former husband came. It was the last event we would ever go through with some semblance of a family.

I wondered afterward if the person who hit the dogs knew this was the final straw, the final tragedy of the family on North Irish Road. I wondered why they didn't stop. Why didn't they care enough? Didn't they know this was someone's family? We would have forgiven them, regardless of how clumsily they confessed. But they didn't stop.

It's like my divorce. I wondered, *Why don't more people stop or even slow down for you? Why doesn't the world stop?*

YOUR SORROW IS NOT IN VAIN

I wish people only had to deal with one crisis at a time in life. Divorce can be all consuming on its own. But we have to deal with multiple issues along with the divorce. It makes life so unbearable at times. Life doesn't stop to let us get through this crisis. I wish it did, just to let us get our bearings. But the world keeps turning, rush hour traffic keeps rushing, and the bills keep demanding to be paid.

Grief takes time. And you need to sit in the pool of grief and allow the waves to rush over you with their powerful motion so they can pass on and away from you. The trick is to not let the waves overwhelm you so long that you cannot breathe. You will gain dry ground, but the waves of grief will come again, and you must sit in the pool of grief awhile longer. But eventually, the waves stop, and you can then observe the pool from outside instead of drowning from within.

Things happen that compound our grief during this time and life seems to break down our spirits even further. What value can there be in this, allowed by a loving God who we're told wants the best for us? To have life stripped away until the only thing left is our bare, vulnerable soul? Welcome to grief. It tears away all of the facade around us. It forces us to see the harshness of reality and reveals our desperation to look up for a source of hope. Through it all, I must say, God never let me down—through all my grief or in any other part of my life. So why the dogs? I don't know. Expressing the pain requires a wordless language. My cries rise to a God who knows my unspoken pain, hears my weeping, and is profoundly touched, deeper than I can even feel.

The words of Corrie ten Boom, whose character and teaching have given me so many insights, come to mind: "Hold everything in your hands lightly, otherwise it hurts when God pries your fingers open."[1] God had pried my fingers open.

Throughout the years, I have heard stories of compound sorrows from people who come into the divorce groups. They faced cancers, deaths of family members, financial devastation, rebellious children, and even more as they journeyed through divorce. I hurt for them, and sometimes I marvel at how they pulled through with all they were dealing with (as if *divorce* wasn't enough!). The darker the hour, the more sensitive we are to the light, and the more likely we are to move toward it—if we watch for it and don't allow it to pass us by.

God's goal is to transform us, to make us better than we are now. Grief changes us. But it can change us for the better—to be more caring, tolerant, and loving to others who have their own burdens to bear. We can become more understanding of what is important in life. I am convinced that our sorrows, singular or compounded, are not in vain.

Though you have made me see troubles, many and bitter, you will restore my life again; from the depths of the earth you will again bring me up. You will increase my honor and comfort me once more.
Psalm 71:20–21

Life refuses to cease its challenges as we go through divorce, and as counterproductive as it may sound, you must take the time to grieve.

Why is grief so important? It shows we have loved. It reveals we were indeed connected at a deep level to another person. It honors the person or the relationship. If we don't grieve, the pain will come out in other, unhealthy ways. We will either work through our grief conscientiously and purposefully, or try subterfuge and allow our grief to work its destruction in other ways. If we do not bring sorrow outside of ourselves to deal with, it will bury itself inside of us. How powerful and healthy we will become when we have the courage to deal with our sorrow through grieving it. Then and only then can we truly move beyond it.

LEARNING TO COPE

Coping skills are those methods we use to adapt to stress and anxiety so the stress doesn't overwhelm and paralyze us. Our coping skills may be healthy or unhealthy.

A coping skill is not the answer to the problem. It is the method we use to tolerate, overcome, or maybe even avoid the problem. It can be good or bad, depending on how we use it. It's natural to rely on a coping mechanism for a time. We just need to remember it doesn't correct the problem; it just helps us get through it.

Healthy Coping Skills	Unhealthy Coping Skills
Counseling	Anger
Journaling	Alcohol abuse
Worship and comforting music	Little or excessive food
Prayer and Scripture	Defeating self-talk
Talking with safe people	Withdrawal
Looking for new solutions to a problem	Excessive spending
Self-help books	Depression (anger toward self)
Coffee with friends	Workaholism
Physical activity	Inability to work

WHY COPING SKILLS WORK

We each seek solace in a variety of ways to find comfort and attempt to rebalance our lives. You need something that contrasts the disorientation of divorce and brings you back to center. Your needs can lead you into strange and unhealthy territory. Just a word of caution as you cope with your trauma: because you are not thinking clearly and are seeking a way out of this pain, you may choose ways to avoid the pain, to defy what your former spouse said, or to counter how you may feel about yourself. You do these things because you'll do anything to dull the sharpness of the crisis.

These self-indulgent techniques work for a while. But when you get sober or face the consequences of your actions, you won't be closer to peace. Why further complicate your already complicated life? This is a critical time to launch your future. Proceed with caution and wise counsel to gain the most you can from this painful time.

SINGLE THOUGHTS

- What healthy coping skills are you using right now?
- What unhealthy coping skills are you using or tempt you the most?
- What are some new, healthy coping skills you would like to try?

What follows are some additional healthy coping skills I relied on. If you allow yourself time and intention to use some of them, perhaps these will work for you too.

THE VALUE OF TEARS

Weeping the day my dogs died was exactly what my body and soul needed. It could not be contained, nor should it have been. Allowing and giving yourself time to cry sounds obvious. But if you feel it necessary to stuff your emotions and "keep a stiff upper lip" for those around you or simply to fool yourself, take the time and shed the tears. Allow yourself the time and energy to grieve. God designed tears to release and remove toxins from the body. Crying can bring great relief physically and spiritually. Make those tears an opportunity to draw close to God. Imagine yourself curled on His lap, no requirements of you, no expectations of you other than to be held and allowed to cry. You can be His child, removed from the stress and anguish of divorce. Draw close to Him and He will draw close to you.

You keep track of all my sorrows.
You have collected all my tears in your bottle.
You have recorded each one in your book.

Psalm 56:8 NLT

You earned those tears, and you need them to connect your broken heart to a loving Father God. Use them to release your hurt instead of holding on to it.

SEEKING COMFORT

Seek those healthy things that comfort you. Whatever works for you and helps is good for you. One way I coped was through the comfort of sleeping with my wonderful dog Sadie. She loved to cuddle, and her presence comforted me. Hugging my dog saved a few of my friends a bit of extra emotional wear and tear, and I needed her furry support while I had her.

What gives you peace? Is it a certain person, place, or setting? Music? Theater? Is it the lake or a river? Search it out. Go there and take a Scripture or a prayer with you as well.

MUSIC THERAPY

I listened to endless hours of country music, "man left, dog died, woe is my life in this pickup truck" type stuff. Although it is not my preferred music genre today, I could relate to those lyrics. All the hand wringing and heart twanging gave me something to connect with. Some songs of positive girl power also resonated with me. I found that Christian music helped my soul after the country music helped my head. We relate to music in different ways, using it to identify where we are and where we want to be. But make sure you end with something positive that gives you a lift. Don't let this be an opportunity to ruminate and stay down.

GRIEVING THROUGH COMMUNICATION

The most helpful thing you can do right now is find a place to speak your heart to someone who allows you to talk. Bare your soul and then be there for your children so they can talk when they need to. It is important to keep the communication lines open with your children so you are emotionally and physically there for them as much as possible. Be as honest as possible and explain only as much as they can handle. Hold them tight, especially teenagers, and honestly tell them you are sorry this is happening and they are hurting. Tell them you hurt because they hurt. Acknowledge how difficult this time must be for them. Speak your words gently and without anger or emotion toward your former spouse. Your presence of mind and acceptance will help ease your children into their new reality.

If you are the one who chose to leave, hold your kids extra tight. Remind them of their value to you. Reassure your children it is not their fault Daddy or Mommy is moving out, and they are the most special people in the world to both of you. Any unity between you and their other parent will provide the children greater peace and security. Don't be afraid to state the obvious. Don't just say I love you; define what that means. Dig deep here. It's necessary to explain your heart and not leave your children to their own assumptions. Allowing them to talk and grieve will help them heal so they don't play out this loss the rest of their lives.

Do not lean on your children through this process. It is easy to do because they know so much about the situation. Consider finding a qualified counselor, pastor, or friend for the children as well as yourself. Having an outsider to talk to will help all of you, and your children can get a more objective view of what they are going through. Let me say again: your needs and pain are too great a burden to place on them. It's unfair to impose adult burdens on those young shoulders, even if they are teenagers or grown children. They have their own grief to deal with, and they are processing it the best way they know how. Reassure them nothing they did led to or caused the divorce and remind them of their precious value.

SINGLE THOUGHTS

- How well do you think your children are dealing with this divorce?

- Who else are they talking to besides you, and is that person a healthy influence?
- How are you helping your children cope through this loss?

FRIENDS ARE GREAT COPING SOURCES

I will be forever indebted to the women who walked with me through my divorce. During this process I learned to have girl-friends again. I had become withdrawn and dutiful as a wife and mother, never realizing how much power and healing can come from girlfriends. The greatest thing they did for me was to listen, and the greatest thing I did for myself was to open up and talk. I will never underestimate the power of listening again.

Dorothy was the older woman of wisdom. Darcy and Darla provided comic relief and compassion. Having gone through their own divorces, they gave me moments of relief in laughter and understanding. I risked making myself vulnerable, and my friends acknowledged and substantiated my feelings. Not every woman can be a girlfriend, but when you find one, you realize how vital they are, especially when you need them the most. They listened and, most importantly, they did not judge.

They threw me the greatest surprise party when I turned forty, the same year my divorce was finalized. These friends helped me survive, and they had no idea how special they were to me. Do not underestimate the importance of same-sex friendships. We need each other, and nobody should ever go through divorce alone.

Be aware of your coping skills, and make sure they'll benefit you in the long run. Healthy distractions allow us a break from the pain—to look away from the intensity of the situation for a time. As you use your own coping skills, don't forget they are not the answer. The answer is to work through each stage of the divorce and the emotions of this time.

SINGLE THOUGHTS

- Are you able to be brutally honest with yourself about your feelings, or are you keeping them locked away tight?
- Are you willing to open up to someone and work through this loss?
- Do you have a safe person to grieve with so you can let it go?

SEEKING SAFE SUPPORT

Some people are able to work privately through their own loss and process their grief. For most, however, group or individual counseling proves to be helpful. In fact, it can substantially speed up the healing. Hearing others articulate what you are feeling when you are unable to express those feelings benefits you greatly. There is also a great benefit to knowing you are not alone in how you feel, what you think, and what you are going through. Counseling and divorce groups provide a safe space to let out the pain and receive guidance through the grief—a place to let your heart speak in ways that give you a break from holding it in.

Maybe it's time to ask yourself if counseling would be right for you. Counselors are trained to ask the kind of questions that will give you insight and healing strength for the rest of your life. We all have blind spots, regardless of how emotionally intelligent we may be.

Many people in the divorce groups I've led tell me group participation benefits them more than counseling. Questions come up in group, as they do in counseling, that help uncover past hurts, issues, and regrets that have undeserved power and influence and need to be faced. Some issues are well hidden, and they need the encouragement of others to be addressed. A group provides the context and the right questions for our pain to be managed. They help us discover what decisions we need to make or to understand the potentially detrimental methods we're using to cope with our pain, loss, or disappointment. Counseling or group participation is hard work, but by bringing out what is hidden in our pain, we can neutralize the issue and take the power away from it. Stuffing our emotions or denying their power is unhealthy. Unresolved pain still surfaces in dramatic ways that sneak up on us physically and emotionally.

CONNECTING WITH A PROFESSIONAL COUNSELOR

For many people, one-on-one time with a professional counselor also proves invaluable. If you haven't visited a counselor before, you may be wondering how to find one and what to expect. You can ask friends, family, or a pastor for recommendations, or you can search through local support directories online. When you go, you can expect an atmosphere of exploration without judgment, and you can expect to dig into areas and subjects you initially think do not relate to your situation. You can anticipate discovering you are a complex human being as well as a simple one with basic needs. You will cover uncomfortable topics, but it is there where the gold is. Many of us have issues, thoughts, and fears we need to be freed from and don't know they are there or how to be freed from them. The process can go as slow as you wish. Counselors don't pressure people. The process takes time. Counseling is not a magic pill that resolves issues, but it allows you to see them in a more understanding way. Over time you'll see it is worth the investment.

JOINING A DIVORCE GROUP

Each group is different, depending on the group's dynamics and the leader's style. But if it is led well, a divorce recovery group provides a safe environment to help you process what you are going through with others who are going through divorce. There will be questions and there will be tears. And both are okay. There are silent times, and no one will force you to speak until you are ready. But there is great power in articulating your experience. It normalizes the trauma and helps you gain strength to get beyond it. You may want to visit a few different groups to find one that works for you. There are some wonderful group programs such as DivorceCare or Divorce Support Anonymous, which I created after years of leading divorce groups. Look for a nonjudgmental environment where nobody is giving advice or looking for their next date. Just like you would never go to a hospital searching for your next date, neither should you go to a support group looking for your next date. This is an emergency room of the spirit and heart.

SAVING YEARS AND TEARS

Counseling and group participation is not for the faint of heart. Both can be cleansing when dealing with uncomfortable emotions and exploring this unknown territory. Your emotions have to go somewhere. It is much better for your physical and emotional health to let them out in a safe, supportive environment. First determine if the counselor or people in the group are safe and trustworthy. Then gauge how much you wish to reveal about your experience.

The sooner you address this old painful business, the sooner you can start your new life without dragging along old emotions. You can save many years of heartache and tears by seeking professional counseling or joining a group. Through support groups you will find like-minded people who are going through the same experience and who empathize with where you are. It is invaluable to know you are not alone.

UNHEALTHY COPING SKILLS

Unhealthy coping, as mentioned earlier in this chapter, postpones the healing and can exacerbate the pain. I wish there were shortcuts, but the only way to get through the pain is to go through it. The fastest way to heal is to do the work the first time to avoid reliving the pain for years beyond the divorce. If you choose unhealthy coping skills, you will end up dealing with your pain later when it rears its ugly head again. And it will. Dating too early is one such coping skill.

I look back at the first man I dated after my divorce and wonder, *What was I thinking?* Well, I wasn't thinking clearly because I was hurting. I needed someone to value me, to hold me. He was my healing relationship. My former husband thought I could do nothing right; this man thought I could do nothing wrong. I desperately needed that kind of adoration, attention, and honor. But sadly, I overlooked the truth of the situation. We weren't a match, and his attention and adoration were not enough to base a whole relationship on. I wish I had relied on and sought the truth of who God says I am instead of needing a man to say it.

Many divorced people try to replace their spouses as quickly as possible. They jump into relationships before they are ready. Understandably, you need comfort the most during a crisis. This is a natural and legitimate need. You are vulnerable right now, and you may seek comfort in the arms of someone new. Some people may even encourage you to do so and may offer to set you up with someone. You may wonder what is wrong with that.

The most important reason for not getting into a relationship too soon is because you will not be the same person when this settles and you become a healthy, single individual. You cannot think clearly or comprehend fully right now all of the ramifications of a new relationship. I know this, because I was there. During this vulnerable time, you will have a lot on your mind, and you need a lot of energy to fully heal. Right now, your head (like mine at the time) is not on straight. You can easily make the wrong decisions, like believing you are falling in love with someone who rescued you from loneliness before you are healed. Or you may choose to move in with or marry someone before you are strong, healthy, and ready. That will only hurt the other person and you because you are merely coping with your loss instead of taking the time to heal.

Use this time to focus on, rediscover, and redesign you! Search out what God has for the rest of your story. Relationships change our focus and the dynamics of our lives. And as wonderful as they can be, they will distract you from becoming more on your own.

Generally, relationships begin while you are still healing because you desperately need someone to make you feel whole again. You want a warm body to fill the enormous void in your life. I soaked in the companionship like a sponge, but I was too hurt to be in an honest relationship; I was too needy and wounded. Although unintentional, a relationship before you have healed may take advantage of the other person. Consider the person who will hold you out of the water long enough for you to catch your breath so you won't drown. Eventually, he or she will no longer be able to hold you up. That is the unhealthy part. Chances are you will end up hurting that person. Why? Because he or she may have unrealistic expectations for the relationship, and because you are not you right now—you are not who you will be when this transition is over.

You must take care of your old business before you are ready to start anything new, so proceed with caution on the first relationship after the divorce. Keep your eyes wide open and continually examine your own heart to make sure the reason you want the relationship is not solely to ease your pain. This is also a good time to focus on your relationship with God, who knows you are vulnerable and need to be held.

SINGLE THOUGHTS

- How well do you think you are healing since the divorce?
- When do you think you will be ready for a new relationship?
- List three things that would indicate you are healed enough for a relationship.

COPING BY RESCUING EVERYBODY ELSE

To deny your own trauma and the pain of your situation, you may slip into "rescuer mode" to help others and your children in dealing with their pain. Focusing on everyone else postpones dealing with your own pain. As a self-appointed savior, you may try to make up for everything to those around you while neglecting your own needs. If you have children, you may overcompensate for their physical and emotional needs by buying things or trying to fill the role of the other parent. You hope to shield others from hurt and minimize the disruption as much as possible. You run in a tizzy to try to keep things "normal" and never stop to face your losses and grief. And then you congratulate yourself for handling it so well. You're not handling it well. You're letting it fester until it erupts in devastating ways such as your health and emotional peace. It is not honest. Be honest with yourself. Cope by getting the children the help they need if you can't reach them. Cope by getting the help you need and set some healthy boundaries. Rescue them and yourself by getting help.

While in savior mode, if you have children, you may try to rescue the relationship between your spouse and your children. The truth is, each parent has to save or maintain their own relationship with the children, and the children also have to be willing to save it. Children are smart; inevitably they see the truth, and they know deep down they have to deal with this loss of a parent, home, and life as they once knew it. They understand who is there for them, who authentically desires to have a relationship with them, and who is distracted and sees them as an interruption to their life plans. You can't save your children's relationship with their other parent, but you can encourage it and offer stability by being a strong, devoted parent to them.

The most troubling times in mediation are when parents use the children to hurt each other. This is not a way to cope with divorce. They may block parenting time, bash the other parent in front of the children, or tell the children adult information they are too immature to handle or too ill-equipped to process. Such behavior causes irreparable damage that will hurt their children throughout their lives.

This passage from *The Hiding Place* by Corrie Ten Boom illustrates the point:

> And so, seated next to Father in the train compartment, I suddenly asked, "Father, what is sex-sin?"

He turned to look at me, as he always did when answering a question, but to my surprise he said nothing. At last he stood up, lifted his traveling case from the rack over our heads, and set it on the floor. "Will you carry it off the train, Corrie?" he said. I stood up and tugged at it. It was crammed with the watches and spare parts he had purchased that morning. "It's too heavy," I said.

"Yes," he said. "And it would be a pretty poor father who would ask his little girl to carry such a load. It's the same way, Corrie, with knowledge. Some knowledge is too heavy for children. When you are older and stronger you can bear it. For now you must trust me to carry it for you."

And I was satisfied. More than satisfied— wonderfully at peace. There were answers to this and all my hard questions—for now I was content to leave them in my father's keeping.[2]

DON'T OVERLOAD YOUR CHILDREN

All children need both of their parents. Unless there is physical or psychological danger for the children, do all you can to encourage your children's relationship with the other parent. You will bless them greatly for their future and yours. Every negative word you speak to the children goes directly to their hearts, which are already hurting from this great personal loss. Meanwhile, watch for opportunities to gently guide them through their crisis. They need assurance. Refrain from providing all the solutions, and instead give them time to talk.

A woman at one of my workshops deflected her pain and stated, "Just help me get my kids through this; I don't care about me." My response to her and to you is this: "The best thing you can do for your children is to get healthy. They need healthy parents doing healthy things so they can regain their own stability. And they are watching how you handle this crisis to learn how they should handle it." I saw her desperation to spare her children pain, and I understood her heart. But you cannot help others when you are drowning. Take time to do your own healing; it will greatly affect your children.

DEALING WITH ANGER

Anger is a natural coping response to emotional pain. The question is, what will you do with your anger? Even when justified it can be potentially dangerous if not channeled wisely. A fire of anger may rage inside you that, if kept inside, will burn you. You need to release it in a healthy manner. Talking through it can defuse it. Vocalize it as you grapple with the injustice that created your anger. Exercise also releases anger, or you can journal through the emotions. The important thing is to find an outlet instead of keeping it inside. Choose to work through your anger instead of letting your anger work through you.

Have you ever seen an angry person you wanted to be around? After honestly dealing with your anger, you will be better able to inventory what is right and good in your life and start directing your energy toward building a new life instead of staying stuck in the past with your anger.

John, a man in my divorce group, kept his head bowed and remained quiet during the first few weeks of group. He contributed nothing to the discussion, until we got to the subject of anger. Raising his head slowly and deliberately, he spoke to the group: "Of course I'm angry. If I'm not angry then I have to face the pain. Anger is the only way to protect myself."

Anger is a natural defense. However, it is necessary to face the pain and resolve the anger. You can deny it, avoid it, or mask it for only so long, but at some point you have to deal with it.

Divorce sparks anger. There are many things to be angry about. Your life has been changed forever, and you feel the injustice through your anger. When we experience loss or betrayal, we feel angry. You may find yourself directing anger at all the wrong places and people, even toward yourself. Open conversations and therapy may be necessary to face all that comes at you in divorce. Therapy sometimes brings out things you don't want to know. But recognizing and dealing with those tough issues allows you to move on with your life and leave the pain behind.

Our society makes it easier for men to deny their emotional pain and considers anger as more acceptable. Ninety percent of the people attending the divorce groups I facilitate are women. They attend because they generally get in touch with their emotions more readily and typically can lay them out and deal with them easier than men can. Because of this, women may fare better in dealing with divorce. Women usually have a better social and emotional network to draw from, and they're more likely to allow themselves to reach out for help. However, even women who believe they are in touch with their emotions will discover things that are unknown and need to be dealt with. The healthiest men I've known are those who sought counseling. They tackled it head on, dealing with feelings of anger, pain, and forgiveness after their divorce. So whatever means you select, deal with your emotions of anger so your emotions don't deal with you.

THE ROLE OF FORGIVENESS IN HEALING

According to Ron Nydam, professor of pastoral care at Calvin College, 90 percent of pastoral therapy is helping people forgive the people who hurt them.[3] People withhold forgiveness for many reasons. Some feel a sense of power over a situation as long as they don't forgive the person who hurt them. If only this were true. It is not. We hurt ourselves by holding tight to the injustice and pain done against us, mentally reliving it time and again, and scheming and dreaming of how to best retaliate, while the other person is out living life. You should be living life too, unleashed from the burden of this offense.

Please understand I am not minimizing the pain inflicted upon you or the injustice that should have never happened. I am just saying it is too big for you to carry, and it will harm you if you shoulder it too long. Let Jesus take it off your shoulders and to the cross.

I am not insisting that you forgive right this minute. I am only stating that sometime soon, forgiveness will be necessary for *your* growth and survival. When you forgive anyone who has wronged you, you give yourself the freedom to move on. It doesn't mean giving them full access into your life; it does mean you remove the need for justice to come from you. Instead, you allow God to administer the justice if it is an emotional or spiritual offense. You let it go so you can make room for your new life and your new dreams and goals. The one who hurt you may never ask for your forgiveness or may not respond how you need them to respond if you told them you forgive them. But clean the slate, for your empowerment and your focus on a future instead of dragging along a heavy and burdensome past.

As the adage expresses, "Resentment is like taking poison and expecting someone else to die." When you forgive, you free yourself. Letting go is part of your healing.

There may be anger and resentment toward yourself for failures in this relationship. Have you forgiven yourself? If you haven't, will you? To heal completely you need to be able to forgive and leave your sins and mistakes behind.

I FORGIVE ME

I wrote the following for a dear friend who felt unable to forgive himself and felt stuck and hurt because of it. And really, I wrote it for me and for you too.

> I stand before God bearing my soul and mind. I am desperate to know peace. I stand in His graciousness and His love for me; I ask Him to forgive the wrong I have willingly and unwillingly done.
>
> God, I no longer hide from you or my sin. It is by faith, my deepest heart belief, that I face my failures honestly. I place them upon the cross

of Jesus Christ to be dissolved in His forgiveness, covered by His death, and removed forever from myself to bear.

You are the only real healing place I can go to. I ask for forgiveness and freedom to let go of my past so it will let go of me. I receive forgiveness and the peace of Christ by claiming His mercy and power and authority to forgive: "For You, Lord, are good, and ready to forgive, and abundant in lovingkindness to all who call upon You" (Ps. 86:5 NASB). You are the truth and the final judge, and You long to set me free. I forgive myself, because You have forgiven me.

Forgiveness of self opens us to receive a new life. Forgiveness of self dissolves guilt. Guilt for past mistakes does not help or heal us. Guilt's purpose is to lead you to a place of repentance. It has no further redeeming value, other than lessons learned from it. There are two places for your sin: within you or upon the cross of Christ. You cannot handle sin's effect upon your life. Christ went to the cross to handle it for you. Guilt traps us in a self-imposed prison where the door stands wide open but we remain unwilling to walk out. I encourage you to forgive yourself as well as your spouse, and anyone else you need to forgive. It will allow you to move on to your new life.

If you protest the idea of forgiving your spouse and forgiving yourself with words such as, "You just don't understand what he or she did!" and you want to throw this book across the room, I understand. Your stomach may be doing flips at the mere thought of what you consider to be lowering yourself to his or her level and groveling for forgiveness. I understand that as well. But forgiveness can be powerful if you make it a proactive spiritual decision. You are not lowering yourself. You are posturing yourself in the understanding of the briefness of life and seeing the big picture of what your life can be. You're making a powerful decision to let go of what is toxic to leverage a triumph. You can stay stuck or you can launch from this place. And you will never launch if you don't forgive.

Forgiveness of self and others is there for the asking. Is it that simple? In concept, yes; in practice, no. But when you pursue it with a sincere heart it is possible. You may not be able to consider it yet, but in time, I urge you to be open to forgiveness if you truly want to heal. Take small steps toward loosening your grip. Watch your words, for your conversation reveals what you are and are not healed from. State your desire to forgive out loud in prayer. Ask God to help you let go of the pain. Throw it upon the cross and away from your being. Let the sun set on this wrath. Forgiveness is part of the grieving process and vital for your healing.

SINGLE THOUGHTS

- Whom do you most need to forgive and for what?
- If you are ready to relinquish anger, resentment, or vengeful feelings, what will be your first step?
- What might your life be like if you were able to forgive and let go?

THE OTHER'S RESPONSE

I was busy in the kitchen the first Christmas after my divorce and turned to see my ex-husband walk into the room. He was with us even though the divorce was final. His mother had just died and it was too tender a time to be alone, so I invited him to join us for Christmas. After spending some time in the family room with the kids, he had come into the kitchen. With a tender heart and tears, he said he felt God wanted him to—and he wanted to—ask me for forgiveness. He was sincere, and I consider myself very fortunate because it gave me a sense of closure. Not many people are so fortunate to get the apology. I forgave him. And I told him so. I did it for him, but I also did it for me.

If your former spouse hasn't requested forgiveness, and you want to forgive, you don't have to be like my ex-husband and tell them. It is not required to tell the other person you forgive them. Their reaction may be indignation or confusion if they don't believe they have done anything wrong. Telling them may only add heartache and possibly place you in the role of victim again. Your actions will display your forgiveness. Your willingness to work together for the sake of the children will speak volumes. Changes in you will eventually be seen. Trust God in this.

Perhaps the one who hurt you will never request your forgiveness. He or she may never take responsibility for any offense or bad behavior. Forgiveness may seem impossible, but it does not depend on the other person asking for it. It depends on you. The only way to sanity through this is to understand you cannot control what the other person does. You can only control your actions and reactions. Free yourself from the painful emotions so you can get past them.

Learn to pry them out of your heart and loosen them from your hands. What will you do with the injustice if you don't forgive?

HEALING COMES IN THE MOURNING

I have watched people struggle when they realize forgiveness is necessary but they're not ready to forgive. And I've seen people who forgive during their grieving. I'm not sure where they get their bravery, other than from God who is working great things in their lives. I remember Belinda. She forgave her husband while she wept tears of heartache and pain. She said that not forgiving added too much additional pain. Others in the group looked at her, bewildered, because they were far from being ready to forgive.

Amid the tragic stories of despair I have seen many success stories. These precious souls took the time and the effort to work through their pain and confusion. They searched for direction and answers for their lives. It wasn't easy for them, like it's not easy for you. But I have seen God take what seemed to be nothing in the world's eyes and create fabulous futures from it. I have seen men and women rediscover and redesign who they are and create a new life, some with new relationships and some remaining single. This is not the end. This time of mourning ends with healing.

I met Marge three years after she attended a divorce group. She told me of wonderful experiences in her life. After grieving, mourning, forgiving, and healing, she explored outside her self-limiting boundaries. She hiked the mountains of Arizona, visited New York City's Broadway, and went on cruises to the Bahamas and other tropical islands. She met wonderful people from various backgrounds and cultures. Others I've met live less extravagantly but find joy in small trips to quaint cities, the lake, historical places, and coffee shops. They learned more about themselves and this new life when they discovered new places. More important than the places they went were the opportunities they gained by being open to a new life.

For me, restoring my love of the arts and culture was a thrill, and taking risks such as joining an improv troupe and getting lead parts in community theater created a fabulous life. There are blank pages in your life storybook. Get ready to experiment and write! God has plans for you, "plans to prosper you and not to harm you, plans to give you hope and a future" (Jer. 29:11).

There will be days when you'd rather just pull the covers over your head and call it quits. Be kind to yourself when you've had too much. Give yourself the time to mourn. The amount of time needed to grieve varies for each of us, and it's never as fast as we wish. This too shall pass and better days will come. Grieving happens inside you (psychologically, emotionally, and spiritually); mourning is the outward action of grief (tears, talking with someone, counseling, journaling, etc.). Both are important. Allow yourself full grief and full mourning for a time. Your soul is begging to release the pain you've experienced.

The healing process is not a smooth progression but a continual work, at times a bumpy, up-and-down process. At one moment you feel good, and an hour later you may feel totally alone because the reality of the situation overwhelms you.

Healing requires you to act before it's comfortable and probably before you feel ready. Through active steps toward healing you learn to release the pain. No one shows you how to grieve. If you listen carefully your body will naturally tell you, but it is easy to squelch the signals, to feel you have to be a brave trouper, a survivor. This is especially true when children depend on you. Allowing yourself time to grieve is important for your mental health. It also shows your children that grieving is a necessary part of life. Even twenty years after my divorce, I grieve in a different way, but I do grieve this substantial loss. Thankfully, I now have a different perspective.

SINGLE THOUGHTS

- Have you had days when you want to pull the covers over your head and call it quits? How did you help yourself through the feeling?
- What kind of progress do you think you have made since your divorce or when you first realized you were headed for divorce?
- What visions do you hold for better days and a better future?

FAITH FOR THE JOURNEY

My Christian faith was a vital part of my healing. My personal faith in Jesus Christ caring for me and providing for me anchored me during the divorce and throughout my life. It was vital for me to know God understood my calamity and I was not alone. I found comfort in the book of Psalms and claimed verses that gave me strength. I took them as proof He had a purpose and a plan. Some people run away from their spirituality during painful times. In their confusion they may direct their anger and blame toward God.

Angela, for example, was angry with God. She was angry God allowed her pain. She knew God controlled everything! *God could have changed his heart*, she thought. Her feelings were raw, honest, and real. God understands what rejection is like. He is rejected all the time. It's not in His character to force people to love. Love for people and for God is a choice.

I wish God would change Angela's husband's heart and the hearts of others who throw away their sacred marriage for temporal pleasure or to relieve an unhappy state. But even in this perplexing time, trust God who loves you with an unchanging love. God gives us the free will to love or reject Him. If He doesn't force us to love Him, He will never force someone to love us. But He does love us, and we can rest in His personal promises of guidance. Thankfully, we don't have to figure it all out now. The advice in Proverbs is comforting: "Trust in the LORD with all your heart and lean not on your own understanding; in all your ways acknowledge Him and He shall direct your paths" (Prov. 3:5–6 NKJV). Isn't that a relief?

Like Angela, Daniel felt God had abandoned him. "You know I prayed for God to be near me, I asked Him to guide and help me, and I don't feel Him answer my prayers," Daniel confessed in the divorce group. I thought about Daniel's comments and looked around at this group. They had bonded together and supported Daniel at his time of deepest need, when his wife told him (after twenty-four years of marriage) she was a lesbian. I recognized how this group was instrumental in his healing and finding life again.

I gently asked, "Daniel, I can't help but wonder if God hasn't answered your prayers by bringing you into this group when I see the support and love you've received here. Could this be how God has answered your prayer?"

Don't put God in a box as to how He will respond to your need. He may surprise you. Keep your eyes open and your prayers rising. God will show up. He longs for relationship with you in real ways with real messages beyond what you've ever seen before, because your need has never been like this before. For me, God was an intimate and a major part of my healing process, directly through His Word and His Spirit's comfort, and indirectly through people.

Christine, like many others, found Jesus through her divorce and discovered a greater purpose that now guides her life. From what I have seen, the majority of the time divorce brings a heightened spiritual experience, because during this season God can come the closest to your soul. Allow Him to draw near you and provide a source of spiritual input that feeds you and meets your needs. If your church is not ministering to you during this time, find one that does.

SINGLE THOUGHTS

- How has your faith been a support for you, or how can you find ways to nourish it so that it can be?
- What have you done for yourself to assist in your own healing?
- What wisdom or insight from this chapter applied to your life will help you heal and move on?

4

ASSESSING AND ACCEPTING

The power to question is the basis of all human progress.

Indira Gandhi

"I don't know what's going to happen to me. I've been a stay-at-home wife and mother, and I'm afraid," Lindsey confessed to the group. Her husband had left the marriage for his coworker. Fear of her future and her children's future nearly paralyzed Lindsey.

Mark, another member of the group, expressed his anxiety through depression. He feared there was nothing left of his life since his wife left. He gave up hope. That is a scary place to be. Mark's depression disoriented him, and he could not get his bearings. I was amazed he found his way to group. It takes courage to join a group of strangers at your most needy and vulnerable time. This difficult state is where Lindsey and Mark began their journeys, but this is not where they stayed.

Like Lindsey and Mark discovered, you have to know where you are now in order to know where you need to go. They had to identify where they were in their feelings, fears, and fury. Facing divorce, you may feel disoriented, abandoned, and lost. Orienting yourself and discovering where you are now requires careful assessment. Your head may spin with questions, choices, and self-doubt.

- *Where do I go from here?*
- *What's going to happen to me?*
- *How do I pick up the pieces of my life, and where are all the pieces?*

These insecurities are strangely normal. This is an opportune time to take inventory of your life and beliefs. You have spent a great deal of time and energy on a negative relationship, either fighting it or surviving it. You can get lost in the process. It's time to find your balance again by first determining where you are now in your thoughts, fears, and hopes. Because marriage has been an important foundation of your life, divorce often changes your core values. This is one reason we feel so upended. As you clarify where you are right now, God will help anchor you and help you maneuver through the divorce process if you allow Him. Once you determine your core values, you can begin piecing your life back together and turn in a new direction. Just like you do with the GPS when you travel, it is good to "zoom out" and see where you want to go.

Let's start with some initial assessments to get a handle on what is critical now. Be honest as you look at and assess your life. Personal inventory requires courage.

Ask yourself:

- What must I accept?
- What must be changed?
- What am I willing to fight for?
- What should I let go of?
- How will I maintain my honesty and integrity through this divorce?
- Should I give it a fair fight or is it all-out war?

Other critical questions will arise as you assess where you are and how you need to proceed. Don't overlook the difficult questions. Engage fully in the process. This pivotal period impacts you now and for the rest of your life. What you do today and the choices you make today matter.

The Scriptures tell us, "Above all else, guard your heart, for everything you do flows from it" (Prov. 4:23). Guard against the negativity that comes your way. Guard your children's hearts from what they hear and are exposed to. Be sensitive to the messages you receive from the television, computer, and radio, and the language that enters your spirit. Fill your soul with uplifting and encouraging words, music, and people. Take proactive steps. Don't wait for others to know that you need to guard your heart. If you are stuck in a swamp of negativity, change your surroundings. Visit a church or watch inspiring messages that boost your spirit.

Sometimes ex-spouses want their former spouses to resume social activities so they can have a sense of normalcy. If you have children, your friends, ex-spouse, or extended family on both sides may invite you to attend weddings or parties together in order to project a family unit. I always advise caution in these matters. It may be too much and too difficult for you to make things look normal when they are not. If you do attend such affairs with your former spouse, drive separately and always give yourself an out. First and foremost ask yourself, "Is this healthy for me? Am I guarding my heart?" Of course, you want to provide the children some sense of normalcy, but first evaluate what this would do to your heart and theirs. Would it give false hope? Would it be more difficult to see the two of you together again? There is no set rule, but simply remember to guard your heart.

ASSESS YOUR THOUGHTS

You may be trying to piece together all the reasons why this happened. I suggest you come to a place where you stop asking why. This may be difficult to do when your head is swirling with different thoughts and scenarios, especially if an affair occurred. But asking why won't change anything. In reality, the break-up of your marriage actually may have nothing or very little to do with you.

And yes, this includes if you were left for someone younger, who you think is prettier, has more money, seems sexier, appears smarter, or is more physically fit! Your spouse may be experiencing a midlife crisis or trying to prove something like prowess or youth. Or, for those whose spouse has decided to come out of the closet and seek a homosexual relationship, that choice may have *nothing* to do with you! I know that sounds baffling, because you are the one hurting so badly or the one who left hurting because the marriage was so broken. But people have their own issues we, even as spouses, may not be able to fix or satisfy—depression, addictions, unrealistic expectations, and the out-and-out sin that takes over an individual who feels unsatisfied. That may not help your pain, but it can help you resolve the "why" question. As time moves forward you may find clues and may even learn the why. But for now, you have your own life to restore, and you need your energy for other things. If you are able and willing, pray for your former spouse, but for your own sanity cease trying to figure it all out!

In your assessment, don't try to analyze your former spouse or get information about them. Don't spy on them through social media. It's torturous for you and does nothing to help you heal or move forward. It will only hurt you further. Close the door on your mental wanderings of what they are up to and how they are doing. If you still love them and have spent years with them, this is a difficult thing to do. However, ruminating ties you to the past, causes pain, and forbids you from moving forward. If you can discipline yourself not to think about them any more than necessary, it will help you concentrate on yourself, your future, and your children.

Find trustworthy people who will hold your confidences in a mature fashion. Your sister-in-law and others in your past who might have been confidantes are not the same through this experience. Life has changed. If your friends shared someone else's intimate secrets with you, be guaranteed they will share your intimate secrets with others. The last thing you need is gossip about your divorce, so when around others be mindful of any thoughts that might turn into words, and share wisely. This is another good reason to find a safe space, removed from your usual social circle, to express your feelings and process what is happening to you.

PERSONAL INVENTORY

Are your beliefs damaged because of the divorce? How do you view and react to your world? Are you angry, overly cautious, afraid, and highly guarded? Here are some questions to help you see where you are now. Take your time on these questions and journal your answers to better visualize them. Generally, the first answer that comes to mind will be the most honest.

- Is this a good and undistracted time for you to be honest with yourself?
- How are you handling life right now?
- Can you explain what still hurts? How are you dealing with these hurts?
- Are you angry? Write what you are angry about.
- Are there ways you are sabotaging yourself right now? How?
- To what extent do you allow others to know your feelings, or have you closed them off?
- How are you encouraging yourself when you have moments of doubt?
- What positive decisions and actions have you made through this crisis?
- What attitudes or actions might be blocking you from fully healing and moving forward?

- Are you becoming more dependent upon yourself and God or on other people?
- What important parts of you (your trust; your confidence; the part of you that is a dreamer, adventurer, creative thinker) have suffered from this divorce?
- Is there a subject that you are not willing and ready to deal with right now? What is it?
- What do you need to help you heal right now?
- Who is in your support system?

Questions like these can give you an idea about where you are. Pay close attention to your responses. Write down any additional thoughts that express where you are. Remember to be compassionate with yourself during this time. Talk to yourself out loud if you need to. These things will help you clarify your thoughts and regain balance.

AN HONEST LOOK

Nancy was brave enough to honestly look into her life. She had two failed marriages and two sons who treated her disrespectfully. Through personal assessment and discovery in a ReBuilding Your Life group, she realized men had treated her poorly because she accepted it. Her mother said she did not know Nancy had been sexually abused by her father. Nancy felt she was unprotected and therefore she must be worthless. Her husband disregarded her needs, abused her, and did not cherish her. Her sons were following the lead of the other men in Nancy's life in disrespecting her. With the Holy Spirit's help, she started looking at these events not as a victim but as an adult with the power to stand up for herself, set boundaries, and make changes. And on the last day of class when she stood up to declare her future, she took charge by changing her own mind-set about her value, seeing God's value of her, and setting boundaries. She learned first and foremost to respect herself and not allow anyone to treat her poorly again.

Exposing your inner thoughts, feelings, and perceptions helps you better deal with them. Be straightforward to avoid defensive excuses, justifications, and rationalizations. Some things are hard to face. But no critical authority leans over your shoulder to judge you. This is a powerful time to be more honest with yourself than you have ever been in the past. God wants to transform you for the good. He longs to work with every part of you. He knows your heart already so it is senseless to hide thoughts and feelings from Him. Explore those hidden parts of yourself that were forced into hiding by expectations, guilt, fear, or shame. This is your golden opportunity to change your life and rediscover your dormant self.

PURSUING THE ANSWERS

Being honest with yourself can be hard work. Some of us spend our entire lives trying to avoid or cover up certain thoughts and secrets. If you skim over the questions you'll miss out. Denying our personal issues doesn't work. Issues such as anger, dishonesty, or unhealthy living can result in tragic consequences if left unaddressed. The issues we avoid will surface in many ways and haunt us until we deal with them.

I have seen the damage of anger, money mismanagement, pornography, and depression and people stuck without means to get out. Sometimes people don't admit they need help, but they want it. Pursue help if and where you need it. Everyone needs help at one time or another. Even the brightest and most successful need advisers and counselors need advice and counsel. "Plans fail for lack of counsel, but with many advisers they succeed" (Prov. 15:22).

There is a place to have your needs met and a perfect counselor who would help you. The greatest teachers of self-understanding are your willingness and God's Spirit. Understanding comes through posing the right questions. Be open to this powerful method, and don't worry if you don't find all the answers. They will appear eventually.

Some answers take time to surface, often when you are more able to deal with them. The Spirit of God tenderly exposes the truths you need to understand for your growth. Many times the truth comes out of a good question, as a thought, or as a comment from someone else.

GOING INWARD

Find a quiet place where you can be with your thoughts—your favorite nature spot or the room in your own house where you feel the most comfortable and undistracted. Be open to the first answer that comes to you at a gut level. If you come across a particularly painful point, you may want to set it aside and revisit it later. Realize that once you face and admit your major fears, insecurities, and points of tension, you can take away a lot of their power and bring that power back to you.

FACING FEARS

- What are your biggest fears right now?
- How well are you handling these fears?
- In what way are your fears affecting you or influencing your behavior?
- What things, people, or activities help calm your fears and bring you some relief?
- What other activities can bring peace, create safety, and help your fears subside?

GETTING CLEAR

- What do you need most or want right now? Is it possible?
- How can you help yourself get what you want and need?
- If it is not possible, how can you help yourself deal with and accept this?
- What is getting in the way of finding what you want or need?
- Could you create a plan to make a new life? Or seek advisers for help? What are daily steps you can take?

DEFINING YOUR SUCCESS

- What is your personal definition of success?
- What are the vital components for your success?
- To what extent do you consider yourself a success? Look at specific areas in your life.
- What are your strongest assets and your greatest talents?
- What are you most proud of having accomplished in your life?
- Who is the person you admire and consider a success? What makes him or her successful that is also attainable for you?

BREAKING THROUGH THE BLOCKS

- Do you deny difficult things so you don't have to deal with them?
- Are you still struggling with unresolved emotions from the divorce? If so, what emotions are you dealing with?
- If you are angry, can you articulate what you are angry about?
- How are you expressing your anger? Is that healthy for you and for those around you?
- Does your anger rise up unexpectedly?
- What is keeping you from accepting and resolving your anger?

- Do you believe if you are angry you are maintaining control?

TESTING YOUR STRENGTHS

- What do you feel is your greatest strength?
- How will this strength help you move forward?
- How do you respond to confrontation? Do you need help getting better at it?
- What area in your life would you like to strengthen?
- How would strengthening this area affect your life?

Your strengths are being tested and your weaknesses tried during this transition. Knowing your inner strengths and weaker areas can help you rally your inner resources so you can pick yourself up and move forward. If you see a vulnerable spot you are ready to work on, find help.

FINDING THE PERFECT ME

Many feel a relationship or a new marriage is the answer or solution to their problems or needs. This idealistic notion can lead you into further troubles. I've seen too many people in divorce groups who jump into marriage or the next relationship too quickly only to face many regrets later. I've seen new relationships create more problems than they solve when people are not healed. A healthy relationship requires two whole people coming together. Wholeness comes from discovering who we are in God's beautiful design, which may or may not include another lifetime partner.

If you are searching for the perfect mate consider, perhaps, if you are searching for your perfect self and peace within that self. Only you can determine that. Paul, the writer of the letter to the church in Corinth, mentioned we are better as we are, as single people with undistracted devotion to the Lord: "I am saying this for your own good, not to restrict you, but that you may live in a right way in undivided devotion to the Lord" (1 Cor. 7:35). There is power in singleness.

Have you fallen prey to fantasy and spent many hours and years romanticizing what a relationship is supposed to be? Do you have realistic and objective views of what a relationship really is? I don't say this to discourage you. Your heart may long for that next relationship, and that is natural and normal. But we can spend endless years pursuing this next relationship and spurn the greatest lover of our soul. That ultimate lover, provider, and companion is discovered in a real relationship with our Creator through Jesus Christ.

I confess I have wasted many years pining, hoping for, and pursuing the next relationship. This is no longer the case. I have found ultimate fulfillment in my gifts and talents connecting with a mission to serve other people. Selfishness is overrated. Can your gifts, talents, and purpose in God fill your loneliness? Can loneliness be filled in ways other than finding a mate? Are you weary of so many questions? But better to ask them and clarify them now than to suffer many regrets when time and life has passed.

SINGLEHOOD STARTS WITH A SINGLE STEP

Lindsey and Mark began as very timid, frightened individuals. It was obvious group support was new to them, and they held tightly to their privacy. It took baby steps to expose their inner selves to the divorce recovery group. Each week you could see them revealing and processing the trauma they had experienced. And the group was patient and embraced them in their struggles, sharing their own pain to let them know they were not alone. Bit by bit Lindsey and Mark dropped their tense shoulders and started to smile, and by the end of the ten weeks, they had bonded with the group and were planning events with the others to continue their support. They began exploring all of who they were outside of their past relationships. They started remembering and unfolding their dreams and made plans to reach personal goals. I wasn't worried about either of them any longer; Mark found hope and value in who Jesus made him to be, not within his former role as a husband.

During your transition you will need to be more proactive than ever before because you are fully and solely responsible for your life choices now. God gives you the free will to choose to follow His path. Focus on the inventory of where you are now and what you have going for you. Note all of the good in your life right now, despite your circumstances. Find your attitude of gratitude for what is, even in the areas you want to see change. Take a moment and reflect on those things you are grateful for. Your life is full of them.

Don't overhaul everything at once or take on major changes too fast. Ideally, if possible, keep things as they are for a year before you make major changes such as relocating, changing jobs, and the like. Find those small areas in which you want to make slight changes that will eventually create big results for your life. Discover your potential by stepping out into your world. Be open to trying new things and learning from other people. Once you've assessed where you are, start designing a step-by-step plan that will turn you in the direction you want to go.

After completing this chapter, and before you begin the next one on decisions, dare yourself to do something you have never done before. The discoveries you'll make about yourself, others, and the world can be exciting. Go out for lunch to a nice restaurant alone; see a movie on your own. Take in a concert or attend an art fair in town. Find a new place that brings you peace and claim it as your sanctuary. Look at your world in a new light; breathe in life to enjoy those surroundings. Pursue singleness. Get in touch with who you are and what you love; start to perceive the world as a whole individual.

Self-exploration can be challenging work. Many people are too afraid to go into the heart and spirit of who they are. It is easy to live life on the surface, but it is much richer when it is explored within. This quote from Charles Caleb Colton is very telling and true: "To dare to live alone is the rarest courage; since there are many who had rather meet their bitterest enemy in the field, than their own hearts in their closet."[1]

After self-exploration, you'll be better prepared to make the important decisions about your life, because you will know more of who you are and what you need.

5

MAKING NEW DECISIONS

When your values are clear to you, making decisions becomes easier.

Roy E. Disney

I watched Bill and Louise divide their life into two piles. She wanted the cottage; he could have the boat. He wanted the marital home; she cherished her mother's antiques and china. He didn't care about the china, or his mother-in-law, so she could have that. As they continued down the list, every item went on their own auction block. Trading, bargaining, negotiating. They had to make all of these business decisions while in deep emotional pain. The wounds ran deep—the affair. This last affair was the final straw. Now it all came down to this, separating life into two piles.

I can't help but wonder how such a moment contrasts to when the couple bought the boat or the cottage. I always wonder, *How does it come to this, dividing all this stuff with the attached memories now a sting of mockery?* It becomes a horrible business decision smeared with pain, points to prove, desperation, and survival.

As if dealing with your divorce wasn't enough, you also have to handle critical decisions while deeply hurting. They will affect the rest of your life. The more prepared you are, the easier it will be for you and the less damage it will cause.

You will have legal decisions and property decisions to make such as refinancing, whether or not to sell the home, dividing parenting time, stipulating possession of cars, splitting assets and debts, determining the value of assets, and then verifying those values. It can be overwhelming. Where do you begin?

This chapter provides a generalized checklist to help you prepare for those decisions in divorce. This chapter is not legal advice; it is a guide to alert you to what to look for and what to expect. It can help you prepare for speaking with your attorney or legal adviser. Every situation is different, but there are some checkpoints that can help you get ahead or at least plan some strategy. This chapter is especially for those men and women without experience in the legal world and no point of reference from which to work. I work with many whose divorce is their first real legal process. Divorce laws vary (a lot) from country to country, state to state, and even county to county. So check your local resources to verify how the laws affect you.

TRIAGE THE DECISIONS

Some important decisions must be made immediately in the divorce process, decisions in areas such as financial matters to keep the household running and childcare issues, along with pending divorce processes and temporary court orders. Unfortunately, most people aren't prepared and didn't have time to stabilize their life before receiving divorce papers. So tend to your highest priorities now. You and the children are the priority. Overwhelming moments will come, so keep emotional self-care a priority. Don't try to be superman or superwoman right now. Just give yourself time to make the right decisions that will help you and the children along with daily living and surviving this difficult time of life. Sharpen your intuition skills; you will need them to know how to triage all your decisions.

Now is not the best time to make major decisions, if you can help it, such as selling the house, investing, or rolling over your retirement funds. Put off any decisions that can wait so things won't be done hastily or cause regret in your future. For the decisions you must make now, are you informed about the topic? Are they decisions you may feel differently about later? Get advice. Postponing decisions allows you time to get your bearings and have a better perspective over your future.

Document your financial activities during the divorce. Journal and clearly track the bank transactions, purchases, and all payments on debts. Depending on the dynamics of your relationship with your former spouse, it may be necessary to track phone calls, emails, and texts. Hopefully you won't need them, but keep correspondences close at hand if you go to court.

DECISIONS OF ATTITUDE

The more amicable you can be through the divorce, the better off for all concerned. Determine your own attitude and approach, independent of the attitude your spouse adopts. Emotions are what make divorce so painfully expensive and complicated, so the sooner you can get your emotions under control and approach this divorce with minimal emotions the better off you will be. I know this is difficult. In my experience, divorce is about 75 percent dealing with your emotions and the emotions of your former spouse. The rest is just the mechanics of moving stuff, setting schedules, and signing papers. But emotions can dominate the negotiations and mediations. Hurt and betrayal can dictate how the divorce goes, and it often does. The question is, are you going to play fair or are you going to play dirty? Playing dirty takes longer, costs more, causes regret, and impacts the children negatively.

However, if you can approach divorce as an objective process to untangle and separate all you have brought together it will help you in the process. Your emotions can run high because there are a lot of memories attached to your possessions. Although compartmental-izing your emotions is difficult, if you can move them into *another* process, such as therapy or talks with a friend or pastor, it will help the divorce process. You will not be as apt to bring it into a meeting with your lawyer, mediation, or the court room. This can save you time, money, and energy. I have seen many attitudes and emotions brought into the mediation room. The most effective attitude (both financially and emotionally) is when parties consider this as a business transaction and not as a place to dwell on emotions.

In the mediation room, there may come a time to express some things that need to be said, but the less emotion in this setting, the better and less expensive for both of you. Cry on your friend's shoulder not your lawyer's.

It merits repeating: decide ahead of time what your attitude will be during the divorce and stick with it. Will you be adversarial, nonemotional, or conciliatory? Do you want to fight over everything down to the salt and pepper shakers, debating their value? Do you want to punish your spouse for his or her infidelity or for leaving you? Do you want to be at war through the whole process just to prove something? Are you battling to make your point and get the final attention of a person who has already moved on? Or will you resign yourself to the fact that this is the next step that must be taken and business that needs to be finished so you can move forward in your life? The decision is up to you. This you can control.

One of the main reasons I became a mediator was because of Charlie in my divorce group. He told me his legal fees were $129,000 and they weren't finished fighting in the courts yet. It was heart wrenching. As tragic as the breakup of the family was, now the parties were lining up to financially annihilate each other. There is a better way, and it all starts with the decision of attitude.

Bring your best business sense into the divorce. Be as low in emotion as possible. Start kindly, but be willing to stand up for yourself. You can stand up for yourself without using emotional statements. Speak the facts. It can be a challenge in many ways, but a challenge that can make you stronger and smarter and teach you skills that will assist you the rest of your life.

ACTING IN WISDOM

Jerry was furious his wife wanted out of the marriage after fourteen years. He used every possible tactic to keep the kids away from her. It was the surest way he knew to hurt her. He started calling her names in mediation before I intervened. He vowed to take her to court and call her an unfit mother. He called Child Protective Services (CPS) so it could be on the record to take to court. Rebecca let the facts speak for themselves. Before the mediation was completed, due to Rebecca's calm composure and persistence, Jerry eventually admitted she was a good mom and should have shared custody of the children. Given time, the truth comes out in most cases.

Facts will be your friends. Stick to them. Determine to look back on this experience and know you had integrity and honesty and you were working on your future not focusing on the past.

You also decide how you will treat the former family and friends. I know things can get awkward. Choose to love them from a distance (perhaps from a far distance). They can behave in strange and hurtful ways. They are also dealing with losing you. There may be grief in the mixture, confusion, and a desire to keep peace with their own sibling, child, cousin, niece, etc. Try not to form opinions or judgments of them right now. A time will come later to connect with them if that is the intention. Divorce can bring the worst out of people, but it can also provide opportunities to learn that you are truly loved and a part of the family regardless of the divorce. If this is not true for you, love them anyway and form new friends. In some cases you will need to form new family too.

Decide how you will conduct yourself in front of the children. We've touched on this a few times already, and we will touch on it again because it is critical for everyone. It is a determination that takes energy and forethought. Abby, a woman in the group, told her teenagers when she found out her husband had an affair. I cringed. Those children could receive no benefit from knowing this information. I understand the woman's pain, but spreading it to her children is not helpful. It is just adds to the pain the children have to heal from in the divorce. That is why it will take a conscious decision to shield them from the ugly and hurtful details. Use guarded language to answer their questions; be honest with them but cautious with the details. They should never be a consultant, confidant, or messenger between parents. This is also important for adult children. If a time ever does come when you feel the Lord leading you to share more details with adult children, pray about it and then approach the issue carefully, seeking to ensure you do not share more than necessary and never tear down your former spouse. Your children are unwilling participants in this divorce, and they will be the children of divorce their entire lives. So treat them as the hurting victims and help them through.

Decide if your faith in God is big enough to guide and direct you. Faith is not blind; it is the evidence of things unseen. Use the Scriptures to guide you and ask God for strength and clarity through this process—you will need it. Some decisions will launch you into your new life and some will keep you stuck in place. Do not neglect to seek God's wisdom to guide you through this legal and emotional land mine. God longs to lavish favor and wisdom upon you.

If any of you lacks wisdom, you should ask God, who gives generously to all without finding fault, and it will be given to you.

James 1:5

He wants your participation and for you to ask Him for direction and help. Jesus once asked a blind man, "What do you want me to do for you?" (Mark 10:51). Jesus, God incarnate, knew what this man wanted most, just like He understands what you want and need most. Yet Jesus asks, for the sake of His participation in the relationship, "What do you want me to do?" I encourage you right now, where you are, to stop reading for a few minutes and ask for what you need.

PREPARE FOR MAKING DECISIONS

It saddens me to see women who are inexperienced with family finances come into the divorce group with no understanding of how to gain control or where to begin. Determination is a great ally when learning new skills. Start by asking for help, moving cautiously, and getting wise counsel. Just because you start in a certain place doesn't mean you have to stay there. Anyone can gain enough understanding to become independent in finances and fundamental living skills.

At the earliest possible time in the divorce process, make an inventory of your financial situation. This ensures you know the value of all the assets and debts. You must know the family finances. If you have been unfamiliar or uninvolved with the finances in the past, promise yourself right now to never be ignorant of finances again! Write out your household income, expenses, investments, and debts. Find current copies of bank, credit card, and income tax statements.

To prepare for negotiation, understand the value of everything you own, including your house, cars, and all other valuables. Know the equity in your home to the most recent date possible. (For example, the owner of a $150,000 house that has a $90,000 mortgage balance has $60,000 of equity in the house.) The housing market changes, so an appraisal from five years ago when you bought the house will not be accurate today. Take time to make a spreadsheet or list of all these items. It doesn't have to be sophisticated, just complete and accurate. Know the interest paid on the debts. Take the time to do this before you go to the lawyer. This will save money and help you get a handle on all of your assets and debts and allow you to see it all in one spot. Don't panic; you can do this one step at a time. It may take some time and that's okay.

Prioritize your list of assets in order of importance. This will help clarify it for you and for your meeting with the lawyer. Note the things on the list that you feel ambivalent about and what you do not want to keep. This clarifies what you would be willing to negotiate on. It also will help you personalize and visualize assets and debts.

Then make a list of your spouse's priorities, what he or she will want to keep and is likely to pursue. This will help you prepare before you meet with the lawyer or prior to mediation. The list you create will guide you. It does not mean you will get everything you want, but it fosters a clearer mind.

Marital property, as the law defines it, is property that you have accumulated during the marriage. Ask your legal counsel if the property owned prior to the marriage can be kept out of the negotiation. Inheritance is usually not considered marital property; however, if it has been commingled, such as money received as an inheritance and used to improve the marital home, it will typically be considered marital property. It may be retrievable depending on the outlook of your former spouse.

If you need help, consult with your financial expert, bank, or credit union. Some spouses have been known to hide assets and obscure numbers, values, and debts.

As you make decisions, examine what is truly important to you. Ask yourself: What effect will this choice have years from now? What is my motive for making this decision? Is it for my future, or am I fighting over past hurts? Do I need more information before I make a final decision and take action?

FORM YOUR NETWORK OF EXPERTS

Legal

For most of us, divorce forces us to expand our horizons and make decisions in unfamiliar territories. Because our choices have lasting impact, I strongly recommend finding a guide, someone with the expertise to help you move forward with wisdom. Legal and financial experts can prove invaluable during this time. Divorce generally involves complex legal concerns, and the laws vary greatly from state to state. The choices you make now will significantly impact the years ahead. You will need legal counsel to prevent shortchanging yourself. Even if you are handling the divorce on your own, make sure you have an independent party who knows the laws to review and can affirm your choices. Read every document's fine print and understand what you are signing in all cases. Ask your legal expert a lot of questions until you fully understand—especially when signing legal documents.

There are several ways to find a lawyer. Personal references are the best way. Ask questions to those around you. Typically, anyone who has gone through divorce has a heart for those who are going through it. They know how difficult it is. They may offer you guidance on how they found their legal representation or assistance.

Where are those people? Are they in your church, at your workplace, or in your network of friends? What if a personal referral is not available to you? Search your state bar association website for a list of lawyers in your area. Review their websites to see their experience, review their fees, and gain other information that will provide some confidence in their ability to serve you. Most lawyers will give you a free first-time consultation. Get to know them either by personal visit or by phone.

Alternatively, search for a dispute resolution center, mediation center, legal assistance, or legal aid in your area to find out about the services available to you. Such resources also provide invaluable assistance. They can be found through the same methods you'd use to find a lawyer.

Before you seek consultation, write out your questions. Prepare to ask the obvious questions about fees, anticipated timeframe for your circumstances, and their experience with your particular type of case. Ask them their opinions on alternative ways to settle divorce. Are they open to mediation, collaborative divorce, or settlement negotiations between the lawyers themselves? Anything you can ask to get to know more about this lawyer and how they handle their cases will help determine if they are a match for you.

Is the lawyer a bulldog or a conciliator or somewhere in between? Can they play both roles for you when you need them? Does their strategy match your decision on how you wish to proceed with the divorce?

Different states have different types of legal aid organizations, created to direct and support people in civil and domestic matters. The United States Congress established the Legal Services Corporation to provide civil and legal aid to communities. They offer legal direction to those who have limited finances.

An employee assistance program may be available at your workplace. They often have helpful resources to assist you in finding legal counsel or with other concerns. They may have some recommendations and ideas on counseling, debt management, and other necessary services as well. It doesn't cost to ask and research your options. Some unions may also make legal services available to you.

Check out these options if your finances are limited. You may discover some less-expensive assistance based on income or even pro bono (without cost). The majority of my mediations involve those of limited means who seek services from our Grand Rapids Dispute Resolution Center.

It is work, but don't despair as you do your research. The sooner you search, the better. It will take time and energy and lots of waiting. Work steady and work smart as you take control of your decisions. Find the solution that works best for you. You want to have as much control as possible, so know your options.

Financial

Jeff and Jenny's house was in foreclosure; they still owed $56,000 plus back taxes. Their car had been repossessed and they were driving her mother's car. We can all find ourselves in precarious situations, but when they shared the history of their behavior in the marriage, you could see these people needed education and help. They could not afford the divorce, which added to their debt, but they were divorcing. Finances were one of the major issues in this relationship and a major issue in their lives.

Finances reveal our priorities whether we see it or not.

The next chapter will deal with finances in more detail; however, it is such a large and important part of decision-making, I want to mention it in this chapter as well. You will need to separate your finances early in the process. People can panic, become afraid financially, and conceal assets, so to protect yourself and to be responsible for only what you spend and save, separate your finances. Go to a bank or credit union and create your own individual checking and savings accounts. The date of separation or filing for divorce will typically be the date of reference for separating finances. Money spent during the marriage will not usually be in dispute.

Can you cancel a credit card when you are both on the card? Ask your credit card company (terms and services may vary). You will need to disclose all finances as you divorce. But it does not mean you cannot set up your own personal financial network now.

Financial Consultant

Who is advising you in your financial transactions? You may need someone to help you with such decisions. Search for someone with a teacher's heart not a salesperson. At the very least, find a financially savvy friend to give you some guidance. This is another area of divorce I strongly suggest you do not go through alone. It opens several areas of vulnerability for you. One is the tax implication of your financial decisions. Understanding the tax implications of the divorce itself is essential. You will determine who will claim the dependent children and what this means for your future taxes. Child support is a state law, child support payments are not a tax deduction, and those receiving child support do not claim that support as income.

Another important tax question for you to ask is, what are the severe financial implications if you need to cash in your retirement accounts (which is highly discouraged in most cases for those younger than fifty-nine and a half)? But if you must, there are tax implications and possible penalties for doing so. Know all the implications of your decisions so you encounter the fewest surprises possible.

Financial Services

Who prepares your taxes? Do you have a relationship with this person, or is it time to find a new person? Having someone who knows your history has advantages, but you may want to start fresh and establish a new financial relationship. Are you comfortable using the same bank, credit union, advisers, and financial services you had in your marriage? You may wish to determine this later as you triage your decisions and the divorce dust has settled. When you do, check the rates of checking accounts, pay attention to interest, and research better ways to invest in the short term.

Medical Insurance

You may have to decide how to get your own medical coverage or whether to remove your spouse from your coverage. A divorce is termed a qualifying event by insurance agencies, which allows you to receive COBRA coverage (Consolidated Omnibus Budget Reconciliation Act) for eighteen months after the divorce. A federal law requires companies with more than twenty employees to offer you the identical insurance plans you had when you were married. The employer is required to send information to you to initiate this coverage. COBRA can be expensive, and other alternatives may be available. Consult with your insurance carrier or your human resources department to understand your options. Although most terms of COBRA cannot be negotiated, the cost of it might be.

Don't make the mistake of allowing your spouse to stay on your medical insurance after the divorce through a personal arrangement. This is considered fraud and can get you in legal trouble. The divorce requires you to separate the medical insurance now that you are single.

Other Insurance

It is time to take inventory of all insurances and insurance companies. Shop and compare what is best for you. Take the time to get a minimum of three quotes for insurance on your car, home, and any valuables. You can possibly save hundreds of dollars annually by shopping around when your insurance comes due or as during the divorce. Life insurance will need to be negotiated, especially if there are small children.

Retirement Funds

A QDRO (qualified domestic relations order) is a court order involving the separation of a pension or other retirement benefits during a divorce. You can buy out the other person, if you want to pay the spouse to maintain and not disrupt the account, or accept the funds rolled over into your own retirement account without penalty. Retirement fund distribution is negotiable in the divorce. For example, if you want to keep your 401K undisturbed and pay off your spouse in other ways, you might want to negotiate to give them something of equal value instead, such as a portion of your equity in the house, depending on what is important to you. You are not legally obligated to split the retirement accounts and give to your spouse, if you choose to split the marital assets equally overall, but it is an asset and will be on the table for discussion and negotiation. Laws vary from state to state so you will need guidance through this process.

THE METHODS OF DIVORCE

You have choices on how you will process your divorce. Don't believe the only way to get a divorce is to go through the court system with two lawyers fighting over your life. You can consider several options.

Informal Do-It-Yourself Divorce

Although few couples do this well, one option is to do your own divorce. The forms are available at your local courthouse or legal assistance center. If you can do it, this option could save you time and money. However, two of the main reasons for divorce are communication and money issues. So it is unlikely you could amicably agree on how to divide all assets and debts. The hurt and anger of divorce usually don't contribute to working together on the division of property. But I have seen this option used effectively.

Mediation

In mediation, the parties have a neutral person (mediator) who leads the negotiation and settlement of the divorce. Mediation can be done with or without lawyers. Many regions have a dispute center, which offers services on a sliding scale or free to low-income individuals. The advantage of mediation is to give the parties, not the courts, the power.

If you both can agree on parenting time, division of assets, and debts, you will create a signed agreement, which is a legal, binding, and enforceable document that is accepted by the courts. You may also mediate a partial agreement, so the courts decide only the remaining, irreconcilable issues. For example, you may agree on parenting time and custody but not on division of property. In that case, the judge would accept your partial agreement and make determinations on the property.

Mediators do not give advice or make decisions; they help you express your needs and listen to the other party's needs. They ask creative questions to find resolutions and facilitate reaching an agreement on divorce-related issues.

Collaborative Divorce

Collaborative divorce is a less-common option than mediation and going to court. Both parties and lawyers commit in writing to resolve the case without going to court especially when children are involved. They hold a series of meetings to work out the issues. Typically a mental health professional serves as the "divorce coach" through the process. They may bring in other counselors, financial professionals, or child psychologists if the parties and lawyers feel it's necessary. The downside is if you do not reach agreements, you are required to start over with new legal representation and go to court. This ensures the legal representation does not have all the potentially harmful information on the other party when in court. The collaborative divorce option may make the risk, time, and cost of this venture higher than mediation or do-it-yourself divorce, but it is also a way to get through the divorce without going to court.

Negotiations between Lawyers

In some instances, the lawyers negotiate without the parties present. One lawyer draws up a proposed agreement, and from there the parties work together and exchange ideas for changes through independent consultation with their lawyers. Several rounds of agreements occur until a settlement is reached. This option requires many billable hours of legal fees to reach a final decision.

Mediation, collaborative divorce, and negotiation between lawyers are options that can work well in abuse situations, so the abuser and abused do not have to be in the same room. I have "shuttle" mediated many times. I shuttle back and forth to each party so they don't have to face each other. The purpose is to keep everyone safe and power balanced.

Court

If discussion, mediation, and negotiation do not settle all divorce issues, the settlement goes to a court with lawyers, and a judge will make the decisions. In the courtroom, your divorce becomes adversarial, and you risk losing more than you bargained for. In this setting, there can be more fighting and drama. Your private business airs in public. It is and should be the last resort. In Michigan, many judges order cases to mediation first, so they only go to court if the mediation fails. This lightens the court system's load and returns authority to the parties involved. Sometimes in mediation people throw up their hands and say, "Forget it, we'll let the judge decide." This takes matters out of their control, and the judge will indeed decide. If this happens in your case, be aware that the judge may not decide in your favor or in your spouse's favor. You may get a decision neither one of you like.

DECISIONS ABOUT THE CHILDREN

Decisions regarding the children should be *for* the children. Keep their best interests at heart. It is vital to their survival and emotional health and yours. Your parental behavior through divorce is so critical because of how it will affect the children. So many times I have seen women in particular (though sometimes men too) feel powerless in the divorce, so they leverage whatever is closest to them to gain power. Often they use the children—either access to them or information about them—to this end, and it only harms the children. I cannot stress this point enough: this divorce will pass, but if you are not careful the wounds upon your children's hearts may take a lifetime to heal. I have had grown people in my groups deeply affected by their own parents' divorce. One woman said, "I'm not even over my parents' divorce and here I am facing my own!" A man echoed that thought saying, "I said I would never do what my parents did to me, but here I am."

Let your children be children without them having to face more detail and drama than necessary. This breaks their hearts regardless of their age. Among other things, their history is being destroyed. Their losses are great. Help them through by guiding them while giving the least amount of information necessary. So many parents use their children as sounding boards, therapists, or allies. There is no side to choose. They need both parents. Please stop if you practice any of these behaviors. You will save your child and yourself further emotional damage.

Some parents swing the other way and feel an incredible burden and guilt from the divorce. The greatest thing you can do is to make sure your children are talking to someone who is emotionally healthy, someone who can be proactive in their lives and available to them. Listen to them as they express their fears, hurts, and concerns. Listen with open ears and eyes, your full attention, and your body language relaxed. Ask them gentle questions to help them process what is happening to them. Decide to be the stable force in this chaotic time so they have someone to hold on to who won't be shifting and wavering. Protecting and guarding them from the dirty details of the divorce doesn't mean you can't reveal your hurt, disappointment, and grief in a mature and honest way. Being real with them allows them to be real in their grief as well.

Child Custody and Parenting Time

I write here under the assumption that both parents are good parents and want custody and parenting time. If there is abuse or neglect, the terms would be different and there is advice that follows. But if both parents love and care for their children, then both will participate in continuing to raise the children and in determining where the children should live. Be less concerned about equal time with each parent. Care more about the school schedule and what is the best environment to allow your children to grow up healthy and safe. How will your actions add to or minimize the children's stress? Where are the children most comfortable and stable?

Child Support

States vary on the child support systems they use, but child support is the law nationwide. The governmental system can be optional if both parties agree to child support on their own. They may opt in or out whenever they wish, with the exception of children on public assistance who will automatically be part of the state child support system.

Different factors determine child support—time with children and the variance of income between the parents. Each state uses a calculation method to determine the amount of support. The courts usually require the home to be as close as possible to the previous two-parent home. The courts can access either parent's payroll wages or business income, as well as personal and individual business accounts. If child support payments are not made, the courts are authorized to affect credit scores by an automatic 150 points. To willfully fail to support your children is considered a felony and subject to federal prosecution.

Custody

Legal custody grants a parent the right to make important, long-term decisions regarding their children in areas such as education, medical and dental care, and religious upbringing. It gives full access to all medical and school records as well. Typically in the cases I mediate, there is joint legal custody, meaning both parents share equal legal authority over the children.

Physical custody means a parent has the right to have the children live with him or her. Joint physical custody allows both parents generally equal time. If one of the parents has temporary housing such as a small apartment without means to accommodate the children, they may have temporary arrangements until the parent gets established to share joint physical custody.

Scheduling Parenting Time

When creating a parenting time schedule, a visual reference helps. Create calendar pages, one for the school year and one for summer, noting holidays and special occasions. The more detail you can give to this schedule, such as who drives the children at what times, the less opportunity for misunderstandings and confrontation with the other parent. There will be times to be flexible with occasional variations such as sporting events, birthday parties, etc. Work together to benefit your children.

Parental Neglect and Abuse

What course of action do you have if your spouse is neglecting or abusing your children? If you or your children are in danger, consider ways to remove yourself and your children from the situation. If you don't know how to get to safety or aren't able to research your options at home or by phone, find a safe environment. The library may be the best and the most neutral place. Use their computer through a newly created account and not your personal account to avoid any traceable activity. Search the options and help available in your community. Almost every mid- and large-size city has an organization that provides a safe haven for abused women or men and will shelter children. These facilities can also help you report a crime or other harmful behavior without endangering your children or yourself. If you fear for your life, contact the police (911) or CPS.

What is abuse or neglect? Do you wonder if the other parent is abusing or neglecting your children? If so, in what areas? Do you see or know of insufficient housing or physical harm? Do your children display signs of emotional abuse? Do they have clean clothing and sufficient food, or are they unsupervised at home? Is there alcohol or drug use around the children? To what degree are they exposed to it? These are all things to consider. Do you need a Personal Protection Order (PPO) that demands the other parent stay a certain distance away from you or the children? Would getting one create a risk for you? It can be a dangerous time if the spouse is angry and volatile. Consult authorities and have escorts if you consider these moves. Do not, however, use a PPO as a tactic to hurt your spouse if it is not warranted.

If your children are not being abused or neglected but you disagree with your former spouse's parenting choices, you may not have any control over the situation during their parenting time. If they play music you know is a bad influence on your teenagers or they feed the children a diet of only macaroni and cheese for a solid week straight, again, as strongly as you may feel about it, you cannot control it. If the children have a medical situation and the other parent's choices may harm them, you can intervene by contacting authorities, but not simply because you are opposed to the choice. This can be a difficult revelation. Jolie watched in anguish as her husband, who used to lead the children in Bible studies, now took the teenagers to Marilyn Manson concerts. His decision was contradictory, but it was also nothing Jolie could control or do anything about.

If your former spouse introduces your children to a new girl-friend or boyfriend two weeks after the divorce is final, unfortunately you cannot control it. Your ranting will not help anyone. Here's what you can do. You can be a consistent and healthy parent in your care of the children. Promise yourself and God you won't do harmful things to them. They need and long for consistency right now even though they cannot articulate it. Pray over your children. If you can be the anchor, the stable force, you will offer stability regardless of what the other parent is doing.

Children are smart. They know who is there for them and who is not. If the other spouse is the "fun dad" or "fun mom" who only spends time playing with the children while you do all the hard work and discipline, you have to choose to see the big picture. Understand you are raising children to be good, healthy people, and your consistency and level-headed approach to this life transition will pay off in great measure. Do what you can, and don't stress over what you cannot control, which will only harm you, hurt the kids, and do nothing to change your former spouse. Reserve your energy for more productive things.

NEGOTIATION

Negotiation is an important part of going through divorce. In the negotiation, like in other moments during divorce, be as unemotional as possible so you can move forward. Negotiating will be necessary for your survival during the divorce and in general as a single person.

As a child, I traded marbles, pocket-sized toys, trinkets, and other silly things. I remember getting some things that I wanted, like boulder marbles and fancy glass jars. Now, in hindsight, I realize it was just different junk from what I already had. But I wanted that junk, and I knew getting it depended on how I asked for it. I had solid skills to make my case for a trade in a way that convinced those who had what I wanted. I had to be nonconfrontational and cordial.

Negotiation requires good communication and persuasion. What are your strengths in negotiation? Can you explain yourself in a way that aligns with *their* way of thinking? You must turn your ideas into convincing arguments for their consideration. Don't corner yourself by threatening them or being unreasonable to work with. Being inflexible, unwilling to hear and consider the other side's perspective, or being harsh and demeaning will only slow and complicate the process.

Understand why you want what you are requesting and present it in a way that might convince the other person. Tie your request into their desires and needs. For example, you want the cottage on the lake or heirlooms or anything of high value in the family. You could say, "I know this has been a huge headache for you to maintain, and the payments would be a burden." Don't say, "Because I know you can't afford it," or any negative statements that could be volatile.

Many dynamics impact divorce negotiation—guilt; greed; self-preservation; ideas of what is right, wrong, and fair—and it is all infused with good and bad memories. I've heard people speak out of so much pain in mediations, especially if infidelity occurred. You can hear and see the pain.

Did you cause pain in the marriage? Would an apology get you further in negotiation than avoiding the issue that destroyed or damaged the marriage in the first place? I am not suggesting you say trite or pious things to get your way. I'm saying to own up to your part in harming this holy relationship if you need to. Change the dynamics by being humble; take responsibility for your actions and your part if it will change the dynamics of the negotiation. Do it sincerely.

I had a mediation case scheduled at the courthouse, due to domestic abuse in the past and a PPO was in place. Domestic abuse cases are rarely mediated and can be quite volatile, so they are often held in the courthouse. I used extra precaution and care in my language. Halfway through the mediation, as we discussed the property, we came to their ATV. Although they had been bickering back and forth on things of less value, the energy instantly changed. I am not sure why this was a trigger, but this tough-mannered, tattoo-abundant man began to cry. "I'm sorry," he said through tears. "I didn't mean to hurt you. Please take the ATV." Then her tears began to flow, as if this vehicle held some great symbolism in their relationship. They held hands as they wept. I sat in silence and allowed the pain to be revealed as he owned his responsibility in the failure of the marriage. She said she forgave him but also made it clear the divorce was still happening because she had to protect herself. Maybe someday, if he dealt with his anger issues, there might be possibility for further reconciliation.

I never understood what the significance of that ATV was or why it triggered the apology, nor did I need to. All I knew was it held some special memories of the relationship between the two of them, and in acknowledging responsibility they could begin to heal.

I'm not saying to become a doormat. If you don't have a history of standing up for yourself, do it now. Take it as a challenge to take control of your life. Speak up for what you want with strength and conviction. Find ways to trade something you don't value as much for something you value more. Be flexible but not so much so other people tie you up in knots.

But you also don't want to be the bully in the room. Listen to the offers presented in negotiation; consider all that is on the table. If you can't get all you want, can you get most of what you want?

In their book *Getting to Yes*, authors Roger Fisher and William Ury coined the term BATNA (best alternative to a negotiated agreement), and it's used often in negotiations.[1] When you come to an impasse, it is time to take your next best choice. Be careful of staking your claim and demanding all of what you want and nothing less. You may lose the ground you're standing on. If you can't have the house, can the other party buy you out of the house? Can you decrease your equity value in the home or trade it for a payment from the retirement account and agree not to pursue any claim in that retirement fund later? Are you willing to give up some stability in your future to have the house now? There are many ways to look at the options and get what you want. Refer to your list of asset priorities. Let your list direct you in negotiation to get to what you need, and maybe your BATNA is the best option.

These are only some of the decisions you will face. Don't get overwhelmed. Look at one thing at a time, one day at a time. Some days it will be one hour at a time and that's okay. Move at your most knowledgeable pace. Consider different perspectives and not just the most obvious.

In my divorce, the house value had a discrepancy. His estimation came from his best guess and both of our emotions. I paused for a moment. *Is he estimating? And if he is guessing, is he guessing wrong?* I was so used to trusting his word. His word had always been good. Tragically, I couldn't do that anymore. He wasn't a safe person, and I had to remember that, even if he wasn't intentionally trying to harm me. Even if it was his sincere best guess at the time, he had no incentive to make sure I got the fairest possible deal. So I decided to get my own appraisal. I double checked the value and stood up for myself. My official appraisal was $36,000 less than he thought. Since I was keeping the house, this made a huge difference for my future. So get appraisals! Make sure they are accurate and from qualified sources.

CHOOSING TO LET THINGS GO

The time will come (often before you're ready) when you will face major decisions such as whether or not to keep the house. It's a common question, and I remember it was a critical one for me. Our home was a beautiful place on eight acres in the country. It was more than a home; I felt like my soul lived there. It was a place of serenity and a great place to raise our children. It was my sanctuary. As much as I loved it, the reality was it was just too big for me with the children growing and leaving soon.

One evening, two years after the divorce, after I finished the four-hour ritual of mowing the yard, I lit a campfire by the water. As I looked around, I realized I was alone. The kids were gone with their own lives, and here I was. I had to decide: Do I keep this wonderful, yet demanding place or do I choose to have a life? I could not have both. Although I loved my homestead and all its wonderful memories, the maintenance was time consuming and expensive. I had to see the reality of it. I had to move through all of my deep emotions and look at the true facts, beyond the past to my future. It was time to let it go.

EVERYTHING HAS A SEASON

Letting go is a skill I had to learn, not only with the house but also with the family I had married into. With the divorce, I became an outsider. There were surprises and disappointments but also lessons on life and human nature. Adjusting to singlehood provides you with such experiences, whether you want them or not. The key is not to dwell on the past, but to see where and how things fit into your present and your future. Avoid holding on too long and undermining the new life you are building.

Decisions you make today require wisdom. Move slowly, stay open to other options, and seek advice. Ask questions of the experts. Make the choices that will bring you peace. Peace is found in simplicity, even in this complicated world. Pray to the God of all wisdom. Remember, He freely gives it to those who ask. "If you need wisdom, ask our generous God, and he will give it to you. He will not rebuke you for asking" (James 1:5 NLT).

SINGLE THOUGHTS

- In what area do you need advice right now?
- Who are some knowledgeable, safe people you can ask for advice in their respective areas of expertise?
- How much time are you spending in quiet reflection so you can listen to your own heart and the direction and wisdom of God?

6

YOUR FINANCIAL FUTURE

Until you make peace with who you are, you'll
never be content with what you have.

Doris Mortman

Jake had never touched the finances. He couldn't tell his lawyer what their debts were or what assets they had. Beth controlled the finances. Jake was at a true disadvantage in the divorce. Not only was he at a disadvantage by not knowing the finances, he didn't know what was important to him to keep. Was he depressed or just unable think from the trauma? Or was he so much in the dark he didn't know where to begin? Whichever it was, his is a cautionary tale.

Many people (both single and married), seriously struggle with budgets and spending. Emotional turmoil can spin our finances out of control very quickly. Over 50 percent of people in poverty are single mothers; so if you are a single mother, please pay special attention to this chapter.

Unless you have financial expertise you will need to take extra precautions when making money-related decisions during this transitional period. I am not a financial consultant, but over the past two decades I've learned that many of our financial troubles are not about the numbers, but our attitudes, beliefs, and unwillingness to put some desires on hold.

UNTIL YOU CONTROL YOUR FINANCES, YOU CANNOT CONTROL YOUR LIFE

Finances dictate so much of our lives it is imperative to control spending so we don't lose control of our lives. It's tempting to use this painful time as an excuse to become "emotional purchasers." In other words, we make decisions based on our feelings and emotional needs instead of on facts and physical needs. We all do it. If you're a man reading this book, you may think men don't do emotional purchasing, but I can argue that point in one word: motorcycle. Sometimes when we are hurting we spend money to mask the pain or because life feels out of control and empty. We attempt to regain control or create an image of a new, successful life by acquiring new possessions, like a motorcycle.

Flashing the credit card and getting what we want now gives us a false sense of power at a time when we feel powerless. But we can't buy our way out of pain. Even though we may think we deserve it, want revenge, or hope to prove something. This is a lose-lose strategy. Amy wanted that elaborate condo in the high end of town. It would prove her lifestyle was on the fast track. Amy got the condo—which she couldn't afford—through a bank that shouldn't have given her the loan. Then the housing market tanked, her hours were cut at work, and that thin financial thread broke.

And so did Amy. She had let her emotions dictate her purchase. Emotional spending will fail you every time if you don't have the funds to support it.

Material things cannot fill the void inside you. If your finances are already precarious, emotional purchases can exacerbate your money problems. For the first year or two after my divorce I lived by the following rule: if I can't purchase it with cash, then I don't buy it. Make that statement a part of your suddenly single life so you won't find yourself suddenly broke.

Once we understand our tendency to allow emotions to dictate our behavior, we can start curbing the habit of "feeding" our emotions. Watch for those times when you're doing it, and try to see why so you can bring yourself back to reality. As I suggested earlier, seek the counsel of trustworthy experts. Look for free or inexpensive options first (knowledgeable friends, books, television programs, online resources, and articles on financial education and management). If you need further advice, consider meeting with a professional or taking a financial class. The money you spend could be a valuable investment.

Times of transition or emotional upheaval are times of financial vulnerability. Be cautious if anyone approaches you with big promises of what their services or products can do for you. Divorces are public knowledge, and unfortunately there are those who consider the suddenly single as potential customers. Be cautious of financial services or debt consolidators who work only to postpone your debt without addressing your financial management issues. It is possible that using these services could damage your credit rating as much as a bankruptcy.

USING PLASTIC

Credit cards have an allure most people can't refuse, and credit card companies take advantage of our lack of discipline. When using your credit cards resist the temptation to risk your future. Interest rates vary depending on your credit rating, but they are often very high, which endangers your financial security. The average US household owes over sixteen thousand dollars in credit card debt.[1] This is a huge issue in this country, so play the game in your favor. Ask your financial expert if you should pay off your credit cards first before you invest in your retirement funds. According to a *Frontline* program on PBS, thirty-five million Americans pay the minimum payment on their credit card.[2] If you only pay the minimum on your balance each month, even at the lowest interest rate, you will never pay off your credit card debt!

The lower the income, the higher the credit card debt is for most Americans. So those who can afford it least are using it the most. That is a tremendous burden on one's freedom. The proverb is true, "The rich rule over the poor, and the borrower is slave to the lender" (Prov. 22:7).

SINGLE THOUGHTS

- What is your biggest area of financial vulnerability?
- What is your current total debt?
- Who is your confidant on financial matters?

FINDING YOUR FINANCIAL MOTTO

Be cautious. Be patient. You'll be rewarded down the road if you play it smart now. Let me state it again: as a general rule, don't make any big decisions during the first year after your divorce unless absolutely necessary. Big decisions include moving, changing jobs, renovating the house, or purchasing a new car or other big-ticket items. Let the dust of your transition settle first. Understand where your finances are now and be a minimalist. Use the first year to focus on healing, self-development, and discovering who you are now as a single person. Money is all about perspective; less of it requires creativity and refocusing on what's important. Concentrate on the things of life that matter beyond the material.

Shortly after my divorce, I was trying to figure out where I stood in many areas, including finances. I attended a craft show, with that pit-in-the-stomach feeling that accompanied me frequently those days. I'm quite sure you have experienced that. Everything in my life was up in the air and uncertain. In one of the booths, I found a small wooden plaque that read "Live within Your Harvest." I decided this would be my financial motto as a single woman. If I could heed this simple advice and spend what I "harvested" or earned, using little or no credit, I could have greater control in my life. Whether that harvest was little or much, I would make it, and I would save myself the financial heartaches and traps that enslave so many people in debt today.

Having a motto to focus on helped me gain confidence. Even today, twenty-one years later, that plaque sits on my refrigerator as a reminder that with the right attitude I can make it financially as a single person. I've enjoyed abundance since those early days, and I've experienced slim times. The motto has served me well in both.

SHORT-TERM PLEASURE OR LONG-TERM JOY?

Budgets are like healthy diets, and I sometimes struggle with both. Both can feel confining and depriving, but each is necessary for a healthier future and a powerful life. Instead of focusing on what I can't have, I choose to remember that wise spending is powerful and gives me control of my life, instead of bills controlling me. Well-handled finances, like healthy eating, will take care of you in the long term and reward you with a healthy life.

To gain a better foothold and understanding of your finances, limit or don't use your credit cards for a period of time. Pay with cash and checks (or debit) as much as possible for the next two to three months instead of using the credit card. This will help you understand your money flow better. It provides a visual of tighter control and assists you in gaining a new understanding of how your budget works. It helps limit those impulse purchases that come back to haunt you. More control gives you more freedom and more choices. When money is not owed somewhere else, it can be used as you choose. And used for better things than interest and bills. Monitor your account transactions online, or use a finance management tool to track where your money is going.

TRACKING AND BUDGETING

There are different options for tracking your bills; the method doesn't matter. Do what works best for you or is the most comfortable. When I was first divorced, I needed a simple method of tracking my bills and getting into the routine of paying them monthly on my own. I used the "chip clip" method, using those clips that hold food bags closed. (I'm quite certain you will never see this method used by any financially savvy person, nor will this system be reported in a financial magazine, but it worked for me, and that was what was important.) I am a visual person so I put all the bills in a chip clip, in order of their due date. When my paycheck arrived I paid the bills. And I thanked God when the chip clip was empty, because it meant I had had enough funds to pay my bills. Assess your system and see if it encourages good management of your budget. Does it need revising? What matters is that your budget balances and your system works for you. It doesn't have to be sophisticated, just accurate.

Multiple systems are available for free or for purchase online that can help you keep your money flow moving efficiently. When I teach Building Your Future after Divorce sessions, I ask people to find a different money management system unlike the one they currently use and plug in their numbers to see if they can learn anything new about tracking their finances. People come back finding either a more efficient system or discovering something about their practices they could do better.

SINGLE THOUGHTS

- How would you describe your biggest financial weakness?
- Do you discipline yourself to avoid the places or circumstances that tempt you to spend money you don't have? If not, how can you start?
- What restraint or financial motto would help you think through high-dollar purchases?

SMALL, DELIBERATE STEPS

I remember the incredible feeling of walking into the mortgage company and making the final payment on my house as a single mother on a modest income. Nothing matches that feeling—no new car smell, no cruise, no bigger house, no closet full of clothes, nothing. The world didn't shout a big hurrah (although I did celebrate). Yet with small, deliberate steps I had gained a major victory. My discipline paid off. Paying off my mortgage gave me a sense of satisfaction and control over my life to live in financial simplicity.

If I can do it, you can do it. If achieving something like this overwhelms you (as it does most of us), just think small, deliberate steps. Focus on the outcome—financial freedom in the future and the peace of being out of debt, plus more choices with your time.

SINGLE INCOME MIND-SET

Here's one way to reframe your purchasing mentality. Compare the items you buy to the actual hours you must work to pay for them. Figure from your net income. Imagine a clock displaying the actual item you are working for. Would you alter some of your purchases? If your car appeared on the clock for sixteen hours of your weekly labor, or your house demanded three days of your life per week, would you still want to make the commitment?

Spending that income boils down to exchanging your life for a dollar. Perhaps you keep a tight budget and already know where the money goes. But if not, this can be done on a spreadsheet or with paper and pencil. When you create your visual chart, make it an overview of that time period and watch your money for the next six months. Adjust according to what you can truly afford. You can either spend your life under the pressure of debt or live in financial peace.

Track every item you buy for the next two weeks—groceries, coffee, eating out, transportation, and so on. Don't forget to add the cost of living—rent, insurance, utilities, and taxes. This paints a clear picture of where your money goes. Can you keep spending at this pace? If you can, for how long? Are there small things you could do without (lattes, dry cleaning, cable, eating out, brand-name goods)? Could saving the money spent on them add up to an extra house payment over a year's time? Can you visualize how an extra house payment could have a long-term impact? Awareness exercises such as this can help you strategize how to change for the long term so you can reap the benefits. If you are fortunate to receive extra income, such as a work bonus or profit sharing, your first impulse may be to spend it on something fun. But if your vision is to be debt free and in control, consider putting that extra money on the principal of your mortgage or into a retirement account, and ensure some security for your future.

BUILDING YOUR NETWORK

If you haven't done so, establish your financial relationships as quickly as possible. (In chapter 5 we looked at how you can get started on this.) Get to know your financial institution or expert. Introduce yourself in person and sit down to talk with them. Build your relationships early. Determine which financial institution is most knowledgeable and experienced. Are they there to serve you? Or are they short-term trained to gain your long-term money? Tell them who you are and what you need from them. They will tell you about their services and help assess where you are now financially. But be aware of what they are selling. They are looking out for their profits; you must look out for yours. You will gain strength by taking control of your finances.

Hopefully your current accounts are no longer joint accounts. If you do still co-own something with your ex-spouse, I strongly advise terminating these arrangements because both of you have 100 percent rights to the account. You have the right to close a joint account. Divide the money and send them their share. From there, you can open an individual account. No matter how amicable your divorce or situation is, I highly recommend you do not use a joint account after divorce.

If you have no credit rating, you must establish credit in your own name. If a loan or mortgage is under both of your names, you cannot just simply remove their name off the loan. You will have to refinance and take on a new loan in your own name alone. This may result in a different interest rate and in closing costs, which you will need to factor into your budget.

If you think you might be running into financial trouble, be proactive. Things happen. Go to your financial expert. Your financial representative may be able to devise a workable plan. From time to time, we all make financial mistakes. I certainly made a few. Don't sign paperwork without understanding the small print with its big ramifications. Be watchful of set up or administrative fees.

KNOW YOUR CREDIT RATINGS

Your FICO score is a financial credit score banks use to determine how much of a credit risk you may be. Do you know yours? The higher your score the lower your interest rates will be. Check your score, also called your credit rating, for free online. Research and correct any errors you may find in the reports.

Don't give your social security number to anyone unless you are confident it is a safe site, as your FICO score and financial status can be impacted if it is misused. Your credit report is a key place to watch for financial fraud. Again, ask your financial expert to guide you through what you do not know. It is vital to make payments on your house, student loans, and credit cards on time. These three criteria influence your credit rating the most. And your bill paying patterns influence your mortgage interest rates as well as your ability to receive a quick signature loan when or if you need one.

SINGLE THOUGHTS

- What is your five-year financial goal?
- Have you created a written plan on how you will achieve your goals?
- What is one thing you can do right now to start working toward your financial goals?

A FEW THOUGHTS ON INVESTING

Before you consider investing for your future, protect yourself by having a cash reserve of three to six months, living expenses saved in a secure place, for emergencies. Then you are ready to start investing. This general information is not legal advice but good pointers on finances. Phil Mitchell, a seasoned and multi-certified financial expert, gives three general tips for you to consider:

1. Invest in yourself. You are the primary asset. The more time you spend developing your abilities mentally and physically, the better returns you will have in life.

2. Pay yourself first (not an original expression). When you set aside funds for your retirement accounts you are paying yourself first. Naturally

your remaining budget is for life maintenance (mortgage, insurance, car, etc.)

3. Have a retirement plan such as a 401K, 403b, simple IRA or SEP IRA plan. Otherwise you could open your own traditional IRA or Roth IRA account. This holds true for self-employed individuals as well. If your employer offers a 401K matching plan, take advantage of it. If finances are tight, let your contributions to these plans drop temporarily if you need to, but don't borrow from your 401K unless it is absolutely necessary. If you must borrow from it, make sure you are aware that if you leave the company, most companies require all borrowed funds be repaid within sixty days of departure. Otherwise it will be treated as a taxable distribution pay (regular income) taxed at the current tax rate with a potential additional 10 percent early distribution penalty for those under 59.5 years old. Ask your financial or tax expert when you borrow from a retirement plan what the implications are for you. Consult with any and all experts prior to disrupting your retirement plans. It is not profitable to allocate 10–20 percent of your retirement income if you have to go back and borrow from your investment savings. Find a

contribution amount that works for you and then forget the money is there until you retire.

The Roth IRA, HSA, and employer plans (401K, 403b, etc.) allow you tax advantages. These plans make up what I call "my old lady fund" for my retirement. You must plan for your future. Don't put it off or believe someone else will secure it. It's time to plan your own.

Financial consultants can help you determine your investment personality and advise accordingly. Some are paid commissions for what they sell (if so, use caution; they may sell frequently to get paid frequently) while some are paid by a percentage of the funds you have invested. If you had already established long-term investments when you were married, revisit your consultant to ensure you trust this person with your revised financial future. Determine if you wish to sever any other ties with professionals who assisted you and your spouse, such as your tax preparer or accountant. If you are considering using a new financial consultant, find out if they have any fines or issues recorded with the Better Business Bureau. You can also use finra.org (Financial Industry Regulatory Authority), a specially designed website to track bad financial advisers and investors.

Once you select an adviser, you'll need to choose what type of investments to put your money in. Your financial consultant will instruct you on how to proceed. Make sure you have a clear outline of your expectations of the adviser and the fees you will be charged. You should make the initial contact with them. Ask your financially savvy friends for their recommendations, and then listen to your gut instead of a sales pitch before you select anything. It is your future at stake.

SAVING FOR YOUR CHILDREN'S COLLEGE EDUCATION

If you have dependent children, you may be concerned with saving for their college tuition. Paying for college will influence your financial future as well as theirs. But don't assume your former spouse has the same views and commitments for your children's financial future and college as you do. It would be nice to assume both of you will share responsibility for college costs but you cannot. If you are a woman whose primary focus has been managing the home, you may also assume the father will pay a larger portion of the college expenses. Unfortunately, divorce can do peculiar things to attitudes and responsibilities. There is no legal responsibility for either parent to provide for higher education. However, a few helpful resources can ensure the maximum bang for the buck when funding education. For example, the Roth IRA and the 529 Educational Savings Plan allow you to save for college costs with tax advantages. If you are in divorce mediation or negotiation and you wish to have some of your split assets designated for college funds, this can be written into the divorce decree. But outside of your heart for your children's education, there are no mandated obligations for either of you to pay for college.

SINGLE THOUGHTS

- Where and how did you first learn your financial management skills and philosophies (parents, spouse, college)?

- Which ones have worked for you in the past and which ones have been detrimental?
- Where is the first place you need to focus to get your finances in order?

NEGOTIATING YOUR WORLD

Financial negotiations make some of us squeamish, but an ability to discuss money, price, and fees is vital in business and in personal life. Your negotiating skills may need sharpening. Opportunities are certainly coming to practice them! You may be challenged to negotiate in areas where you lack experience, such as replacing roofs, reparing a furnace, fixing plumbing, buying a new car, and more. Don't be afraid to ask questions again and again of a sales-person or contractor until you fully understand your options. Try to find the alternatives, perhaps not evident at first glance. Some options may not be volunteered by the business you are dealing with because they're less profitable to them. I frequently see people on social media asking friends and business associates for qual-ity workers who do specific work (such as roofing, electrical, or plumbing work). They ask because they are uncertain who is a skilled professional in that area. I highly recommend asking. This may be all new to you, so boldly go where you have never gone before!

Confronting someone on a price requires nerve. In other countries this is more acceptable than in the United States. But you can save 10 to 20 percent simply by asking. Empower yourself by asking. Practice using phrases like: "Are any discounts available on this item?" "This item is the last one. I'd like to purchase it for less than it is marked since it's out of the box." "I need a better price on this item, would you take X?" It's how you ask that is the key.

Penny Rosema, an international negotiator and owner of TwoViews, a company that teaches negotiation skills, shared with me, "If you don't ask the answer is always no."[3] So ask. Learn to ask. Find different ways to ask. Ask again when the answer is vague, and try once more when the answer is no. But don't walk away from a negotiation or a business transaction wondering, *If I had been a little more assertive, could I have gotten a better deal?*

Look after your own personal financial business. There are times to be proactive and take a creative approach. Does your roof need to be redone? Don't go with the first estimate—get three or four. Choose the lowest bid and take it to the person you really want to do the work to see if they will match or beat the lowest bid. Ask for reliable references or contact the Better Business Bureau. See if there have been any complaints against the company.

You can negotiate with just about anyone—roofers, plumbers, home construction workers, salespeople, realtors, and even sometimes with store employees, particularly if an item is on clearance, slightly damaged, or poorly packaged. Negotiating is a skill you need to know, and it will be vital to your financial survival. It trains you in tactful communication to get what you want. The worst the other party can say is no. It's worth the risk to get one yes to make it pay off.

CREDIT CARD CONTROL

We all know it's important to pay your bills on time. Being late on payments more than sixty days triggers a penalty rate. The added interest penalizes your future. Can you ever catch up?

A higher interest rate means higher minimum monthly payments and more interest. And yet, many people make late payments for convenience or to get what they want now. I realize you may be struggling to get by, but a higher interest rate on your credit card hurts you. The compound impact of a higher interest rate gets complicated so easily. It's best to keep your credit card transactions to a level you can afford to pay off each month and eliminate the risk of a higher interest rate, which ultimately impacts your credit card balance and your FICO score.

The Federal Reserve surveyed more than five thousand people and found a startling statistic: about 46 percent of Americans said they did not have enough money to cover a four-hundred-dollar emergency expense. Instead, they would have to put it on a credit card and pay it off over time, borrow from friends or family, or simply not cover it at all.[4]

Awareness is the name of the game. Details you overlooked in the past will require your utmost attention now. Although you must monitor and be responsible for a multitude of things, you cannot afford to stay uninformed regarding money matters. Minimum monthly payments increase the years you'll be in debt. That "I want it now" philosophy will steal your future. If someplace offers the greatest sale ever but charges a high interest and adds years of payments, it is not a sale at all. Can you afford to save any more money shopping "sales"? Clarify what adds to your life and understand that charging with credit subtracts from your life. You work too hard to give a credit card company your paycheck. Put that same money into a wise investment fund where it can yield personal wealth and security for you.

Keep your money concerns as simple as you can. Especially keep it simple the first few years of being single. Life is complicated enough on its own, so control what you can control.

HOME BUYING

I've suggested you resist making major purchases during the first year or two of suddenly becoming single, but sometimes it is necessary. If you are undecided about what you want to do or where you want to live, consider renting for a short time instead of buying. Or move in with someone while you review your options. A short-term arrangement may be temporarily humbling, but it can substantially boost your future financial security.

If you must make the major purchase of a house, I recommend you connect with a financial adviser, and verify these statements with them. As a general rule, most financial experts recommend fixed interest mortgages because you can always pay more on the principal at any time, but if finances get tight you can at least make the defined payments. An interesting fact about fifteen-year mortgages—in the first year of the mortgage you pay 50 percent on the principal. If you have a thirty-year mortgage, it will take you fifteen years to reach this percentage of principal payment. So when you buy a home, seriously consider only buying a home you can afford with a fifteen-year mortgage. A fifteen-year mortgage may work best if your career is secure and you can make the higher payments. Definitely avoid the adjustable rate mortgage or "interest only" loans. Interest rates on these can change in ways you may not be prepared to handle. Consult with your mortgage officer or banker to know all your options, since every situation is different.

If you buy a house or take on a mortgage, be aware of the impact you can make by adding extra money onto each payment during the first few years of the mortgage. Those extra dollars go directly toward the principal. You will save thousands of dollars in interest and pay off your loan years earlier. That's one reason I could walk into my mortgage company and write that last house payment. The common notion is that you will lose out on the tax write-offs if your house is paid off. You should consult your financial consultant for advice on this issue, but most file a standard deduction tax form so your mortgage payment isn't deducted anyway. Plus, for many people, paying out money to get a portion of it back just doesn't make sense. Again, run this by a financial counselor you trust. The following equations may open your eyes to what I'm suggesting.

Take a $150,000 thirty-year loan at 4 percent interest. Your monthly payment would be $716.12. If you added $50 to your payments for the first five years ($50 x 12 months x 5 years = $3,000), you would nearly double your money through reduced interest payments and save $5,827.00. If you paid the extra $50 per month for the entire fifteen years you would knock off $14,372.53 that you otherwise would have to pay over the life of the loan.

If I pay $815 on my mortgage each month, I will spend $9,780 per year. That $9,780 divided by my $52,000 net annual salary equals 18.8 percent. That's how much of my income pays for the mortgage. Now, consider that as a percentage of the work I do: 18.8 percent of my forty-hour week is 7.52 hours per week (or about thirty hours per month). That's how much I work each week (and month) to pay the mortgage. These are some things to think through when you consider your next home purchase. Is this house worth the time of your life it would require to pay for it?

LIVE WITHIN YOUR HARVEST

The words of Benjamin Franklin are timeless and appropriate for every person, single or not. But they are especially appropriate now, when divorce has knocked so much of your life out of control. He said, "Think what you do when you run into debt; you give another power over your liberty."[5]

My grandfather Moses used to say it doesn't matter how much money you make, what matters is how you spend it. This also includes how much you save for your future. I took his words to heart and practice. I hope you will too.

You might be thinking financial health is not so much a lack of discipline as a lack in paycheck. I understand. Sometimes circumstances don't allow you to budget precisely. Raising teenagers provides a perfect example of when you must grapple with the inexact science of unplanned financial needs. They spontaneously spring impossible-to-predict expenses on you, along with the necessary expenses such as school, sports, and other activities. It is nearly impossible to control those unknown, unexpected expenses. However, by devising a plan with guidelines, you will have something to work with. You can budget an amount for the unexpected. Teach your children the difference between a need and a want. Sometimes they need to hear no, just like we all hear no in the real world. Learning financial discipline will help them become responsible adults as they grow up.

When my children were young, we had very little money. We would go to McDonald's after church and I'd tell my kids, "You can have fries or a soda with your hamburger, but you can't have both." It touches my heart that they recall this experience with no anguish or resentment. When they think of those moments, along with the homemade Halloween costumes and popsicles in the park, they smile at the memories we made. It was good for my children to have limits on their choices. The key is how you present your no and the limitations you set. Teach them discretion as a challenge or a game, and show them the thrill of a bargain. Teach them that life is all about the discipline of choices and keeping the big picture in mind. As Abigail Van Buren, the advice columnist, put it, "If you want your children to turn out well, spend twice as much time with them, and half as much money on them."[6]

I don't know how much your finances have changed, but I rarely meet a single woman or man who isn't greatly affected financially by divorce. I cannot emphasize enough the need to be wise with money at this critical time. Your future is at risk. If you are wise and disciplined, you can make this transition a smoother and shorter one. Again, live within your means, and you will have future harvests to reap.

THE GIVING CIRCLE OF LIFE

One last thought on finances. For balance in our lives, it is important we find someplace to contribute that is greater than ourselves. We need a cause we believe in. Perhaps it's your church, your school, or a favorite community agency. You can contribute time or money, or both. It is not necessarily the amount you give that matters as much as the act of giving. Life is about giving and receiving. When we give to enrich other people's lives, we enrich our own. Even as you watch out for your financial future, always look for and find a way to contribute to something greater than yourself.

7

GOING SOLO IN A COUPLES' WORLD

I wonder, my friend, what would happen if you embraced
that stranger of Aloneness, seeing him not as the Stranger
who has come to take something from you, but as the Blesser
who has come to bestow on you something wonderful!

Cindi McMenamin

In 2016, 109 million single people lived in the United States, according to the US Census Bureau. The population continues to climb and narrow the gap between the number of married and unmarried people over the age of eighteen.[1] If you are a single man or woman, you are in good company. That may not help the feeling of isolation you have right now, but it reveals that you are not alone in being alone. Although we get mixed messages in our culture, I'm not "half" of anything and you're not "half" of anything. We are whole just as we are. It is unknown how long you will be single (it could be permanent), so prepare for living single. And prepare yourself for what can be a wonderful life.

Being newly unmarried can be awkward. In many ways our relationships define us. This is not only a cultural definition, but for many of us, it is what we believe is true. We grapple with this missing part of our identity. This new, ambiguous status may bring back the self-conscious emotions you experienced during those insecure teen years. Remember those times when you were preoccupied with, sensitive to, and insecure about how others perceived you? No one wants to go back to those high school days, nor those feelings.

MISSING THE OTHER HALF

One of the hardest things you'll ever do is grieve
the loss of a person who is still alive.

Jeanette Walls

Unlike widows and widowers, the divorced still have to deal with the person they lost for the rest of their lives if they have ties such as children or work or if they live in the same town.

When first becoming single, it may feel as if you are missing half of yourself. In your past, you had the comfort of having a partner nearby—of having someone to rely on when you were in need. If you faced an important decision, you always had a sounding board. Even if the relationship wasn't perfect, you had a sense of value in being connected to that person, of being a vital part of another person's life. These images stand in stark contrast to where you are now. As difficult as this time can be, it provides an opportunity for you to become a stronger person. The truth is, you will never be the same person after this experience, and it is up to you to determine if that new person will be a strong and healthy one.

You now have to be the one to double-check everything in your decisions. Pain and uncertainty accompany this transition, which makes your singleness feel foreign and awkward. One man in a group I led, Charlie, told the story of how his wife always hated that he fell asleep on the couch while watching the news. After she left him, he watched the news and fell asleep on the couch. Waking in the middle of the night, he got up to go to bed. Then realized, he didn't have to get into the bed any longer, so he went back to sleep on the couch. You will sometimes react out of habit and then discover what you do is now up to you. The awkward "firsts" will come, but the good news is you only have to do the first times once. There will be the holidays and other social events, which can be torturous reminders that you are alone. But I promise you, in time, the intensity will lessen and you will find your own stride again as an individual person.

SEEING THE WHOLENESS OF "PERFECT" COUPLES

As you adjust to being alone, you may notice those "perfect" couples that seem to make a mockery of your life. Don't let them intimidate you. Acknowledge their beauty. In fact, rejoice in it. You are not any less valuable or credible in their presence. The world has ample room for couples and for you too, as a single person. Reconsider and redesign the attitude that believes the world was created only for couples. It was *not* created only for couples. When you see couples, focus on the beauty of relationships not on your loss. Don't shut out opportunities in life simply because you are single. It is time to believe you are indeed a whole person. Accept, cultivate, and eventually celebrate your individual uniqueness and wholeness. You may argue, "But God said it is not good to be alone" in Genesis. Indeed He did. So don't be alone; find a community. Find like-minded people and join them.

EMBRACE YOUR WHOLENESS

It will take time to adjust and learn to appreciate that you are a whole being. Don't be surprised at the awkwardness. It's normal to feel a little lost while you resume your new life. Just take a deep breath, say "Okay, here we go," and step into the rest of your story. Being single does not make you flawed, incomplete, or diseased. In fact, you are undoubtedly, in many people's eyes, the idea of a potential mate exactly as you are. The rest of your story can be beautiful.

One of the men in my ReBuilding Your Life class approached me after class, shrugged his shoulders, and said, "I read your book. I did not like the fact that you kept telling us to become healthy single people. I wanted the next relationship, and I resisted your words wholeheartedly. Then I dated and had a couple of relationships, and now I know what you mean. I cannot have a healthy relationship until I am healed, and I must work on myself to become a healthy single person."

I wish there were shortcuts. But as you go out into the world searching to attach yourself to someone else, your unhealed self shows up and reveals you are not ready. I know no one wants to hear those words, but I assure you I have worked with far too many people who have remarried too fast, jumped into the next relationship too soon, and found themselves devastated again. Do your homework.

Chances are you are doing better than you think because you are doing things such as reading this book. The anxiety will subside and life will settle into a new pace and a new dynamic as you begin to mold and make a new life. Don't forget that God desires to be a part of this new creation; don't neglect Him. He is the God of second chances and new directions. Seek His counsel, His comfort, and His presence as you venture out into your new world.

YOUR SOURCE OF CONFIDENCE

Divorce can cause self-doubts and insecurities to surface. Yet something wonderful can also resurface—your own person, unhampered, unhindered, and unapologetic. Build your confidence from another source—the Word of God, the Scriptures, the voice of your faith. God's love defines us as highly valuable, precious, and worthy of love. What better starting place could there be? Psalm 139:1–18 reveals how God knows, regards, thinks about, and loves you. This time of your life is not a surprise to Him.

You have searched me, LORD,
and you know me.
You know when I sit and when I rise;
you perceive my thoughts from afar.
You discern my going out and my lying down;
you are familiar with all my ways.
Before a word is on my tongue

you, LORD, know it completely.
You hem me in behind and before,
and you lay your hand upon me.
Such knowledge is too wonderful for me,
too lofty for me to attain.
Where can I go from your Spirit?
Where can I flee from your presence?
If I go up to the heavens, you are there;
If I make my bed in the depths, you are there.
If I rise on the wings of the dawn,
if I settle on the far side of the sea,
even there your hand will guide me,
your right hand will hold me fast.
If I say, "Surely the darkness will hide me
and the light become night around me,"
even the darkness will not be dark to you;
the night will shine like the day,
for darkness is as light to you....
Your eyes saw my unformed body;
all the days ordained for me were
written in your book
before one of them came to be.
How precious to me are your thoughts, God!
How vast is the sum of them!
Were I to count them,
they would outnumber the grains of sand—
when I awake, I am still with you.

ACCEPTANCE

Acceptance of who you are and where you are is a vital part of your healing. Accept your value as a person above all and then accept your life as it is now, without rationalization or excuses. Healing requires acceptance of your losses and acceptance of where you landed after the divorce. Accept if you are broken, wounded, or needy. Accept it so you know what to pursue to make the changes you want to make. Until you reach acceptance, you cannot begin to build your life. Until you get to acceptance, you'll remain stuck in the past, ruminating over what once was and reliving all of your hurts.

There are three empowering things you can do with your solo life right now:

- Get help. If you need help accepting your new life and processing your circumstances, find a counselor.
- Get it together. Search and figure out what you want and need.
- Get moving. If you know what to do, do it. And if you don't know what to do, find a wise adviser who can help you learn to find out.

Acceptance is so critical as one of the four stages of divorce. The old life won't fit anymore. Things will be different. You'll be different. Don't despair at that thought. Instead, be intrigued by it and open your eyes to the possibilities. Have you had your garage sale of the home and heart? Look at the material space around you and determine what is clutter that no longer belongs. What needs to go so you can fill your life with new things and new possibilities? Examine your head and heart and do the same. Survey your life now and accept it with gratitude! Gratitude always makes the world bigger, full of potential, and generally better. I've never seen it fail yet.

REDESIGNING RELATIONSHIPS

Major changes may occur in friendships when your marriage relationship ends in divorce. Those friends might not know how to create a new, neat, predictable package of who you are now. They struggle to figure out what a relationship with the new you might look like. This is not your issue; it's theirs. Be prepared that you may lose some of the friends you had when you were part of a couple and certain relationships may change. This happens. Some of your relationships with couples that were once intimate may become shallow or distant. Some people just don't know how to deal with odd numbers. They are a couple; they may think in couples. Be comforted in knowing that in time you will establish new long-lasting relationships.

As you begin to heal, you will find your beliefs changing and shifting and may conclude that some of your beliefs were incorrect. If you were in a condemning relationship, you may have an "aha" moment about your physical features, intelligence, and preferences. Abusive relationships take their toll, but the human spirit is amazingly resilient. If you were exposed to abuse, criticism, and rejection, you may have started to believe some lies or personal insults and lived life on autopilot. But once alone, you can discover the negative things were not true at all. That will be a liberating moment for you. Sadly, as painful as divorce is, there can be moments of relief now that you are single. No one is disapproving of your choices or your life's direction. Peace is priceless.

SINGLE THOUGHTS

- In the past, what activities did you believe could only be done as a couple and why?
- What is the most important way you have defined or redefined your value?

REDESIGNING YOUR WORLD

You start redesigning your world by changing your mind-set. You have to be the first to believe that being single can mean being strong. You have past successes—independent acts and strong character traits that defined you. I encourage you to make a list of those past successes and accomplishments—perhaps you've forgotten many of them. What are you most proud of? Reconsider the skills and strengths you possess, especially those that have been disregarded or underestimated in the past.

Remember those dreams you once had? Now is the time to review and revive them. Haul them out of the attic of your mind and consider them carefully for the treasure they hold. This is the time to focus on you, not to become a self-centered diva or divo, but to find the rest of your story and become strong enough to discover your purpose. And with that purpose you can contribute to other people's lives. Now is the time to redesign your world. You redesign it from the inside out.

SET UP A PERSONAL NETWORK

As you redesign your world, building and maintaining professional and personal relationships are vital. This is your network. If you already have solid relationships, strengthen and honor them. Reinforce the bonds you share with others. Value your dearest friends and family members. Don't avoid certain friends due to your current state. Seek them out and let them know you're still alive and ready to move on with your new life. Invite others out for lunch. Make quick phone calls or write some notes.

Look for good and positive people to strengthen your network. Appreciate those who help you maintain your physical world. Pay them on time, and pay them well. Issues like broken pipes force you to reach out and build that network, whether you want to or not. It is much easier to create those connections before trouble comes, and having them established gives you peace of mind.

You may not feel comfortable right now working on enlarging your network. But you're already out of your comfort zone, so why not? Get curious about new activities and social circles; begin to explore the world around you. Find a meet-up group that hikes, kayaks, travels, or attends lectures or the theater. Open your mind to new ideas and watch for opportunities to learn, grow, and expand your world. Introduce yourself to a new social climate. Join a gym, get involved in a book club or discussion group, volunteer, take a dance class, find an area of study, learn a new skill or language. Broaden your horizons so you can intelligently converse on social issues, literature, art, or other pursuits.

Marta became an entrepreneur. She always wanted to be one but never had her husband's support to do it. So she began working in a small coffee shop to learn the business and is now venturing out to open her own store. The possibilities are endless, just like your world is. Don't allow fear to paralyze you. Build that network to build your new life.

BRANCHING OUT

It may be natural to want to withdraw or hide from the world. I withdrew; I didn't want or know how to face the world. But I had to attend my kids' basketball games and cross-country meets. The kindness and support the other parents and the community gave me surprised me. Withdrawing is understandable, but it isn't healthy for an extended period of time. By withdrawing, you may feel you gain control over your environment and stay safe, but you also miss out on opportunities for growth, adventure, and good things to come. We all need to belong, especially during tough times. You may be tempted to shut out the world, to shield yourself from more hurt. I understand, but I encourage you to do the exact opposite. Instead of wrapping up in self-protection, open up to safe people, safe places, and safe activities. You may look around and see people smiling, laughing, and living their lives. It's time for one of those vibrant people to be you.

SINGLE THOUGHTS

- Have you been tempted to withdraw from people? How have you handled the urge?
- Who is in your personal network?
- Whom would you call in the middle of the night if your car broke down or you locked yourself out of the house?
- Whose social network list are you on, and what can you do for that person?
- What activity or social area could you get involved in, so you can expand your world?

REDESIGNING YOUR JOURNEY

As the first step in redesigning your journey, determine where you really want to go. Do you want to go back to school, change careers, start a career, attend the theater, go to a festival, hit the beach, explore a tourist town, or take a trip? What is stopping you? Are you telling yourself it's easier to stay home? Do you insist the kids need you and therefore anything you want and need isn't valid? They do need you tremendously, but this can also be used as an excuse to avoid creating your own life.

If you have no money, you can still redesign your journey by visiting bookstores, attending lectures, walking the lakeshore, going to a park, visiting an art gallery, or going to a museum on free admission days. Take note of when you are making excuses, then direct yourself into doing something anyway. This could turn out to be a delightful surprise. Your life is up to you, and you will never find adventure or growth by watching other people live their lives. Don't escape life—find it. Turn toward life and its opportunities, and find new things to embrace.

This is your second act, and it can be the best part. Author and founding pastor of Willow Creek Community Church, Bill Hybels, challenged, "Tell me why your next five years couldn't be your best five years?"[2] Remember what you dreamed of long ago, before everyday life and struggles or relationship problems overwhelmed you? Do you even remember what you truly wanted for your life? What got in the way? I know the world may look dark and scary sometimes, but don't let discomfort stop you. Maybe the darkness you see is the shadow side of something wonderful—something that can help you develop, reach out, and live passionately. Seek those new experiences. Opportunities that will help you grow and flourish await you. Find them!

COURAGE FOR THE JOURNEY

Courage is being afraid of something and facing it anyway. It is the result of freeing yourself from blocks and barriers. Don't let fear intimidate you. Yes, moments of awkwardness, fear, or insecurity will happen. You may find yourself brushing tears from your eyes or swallowing a lump in your throat. Step out anyway. Give yourself an out if you get overwhelmed; then congratulate yourself for taking the chance. Stretching beyond your comfort zone can be stressful. Don't settle for a small, routine life. Step forward, pray, and live boldly. Every journey begins with a single step.

PARTY OF ONE

You give yourself a tremendous gift when you learn to enjoy your own company. Pursue singleness; pursue you! The evening will come when you have nothing planned, but you don't feel like staying home. What will you do with this time? Will you flip on the TV and watch reruns, or will you take yourself out on a date? Become a tourist in your own town. Bookstores with coffee bars provide a great place to start. Hang out and browse a few books. Such places offer a quiet, safe, and relaxed environment. Rediscover your local library and other places you pass everyday. Look for lectures and authors speaking at your local bookstore or library.

Take yourself to a favorite restaurant with an outside eating area, a garden room, or tables overlooking the water. Discover charming little towns or museums. This is *your* life. Take it all in with deep breaths and appreciation for who you are and who you are becoming. Don't simply react to life. Make it happen.

BE STRONGER THAN YOUR EMOTIONS

At any time, at any unguarded moment, emotions can sweep you away. This may sound odd, but there are times when you simply must plow through or step over your feelings and not let them stop you. Be realistic and also compassionate with yourself. As you heal, you'll be able to override self-doubt and other negative feelings. I suggest you don't wait until you feel ready, but challenge yourself to do it now. Those insecure feelings may fade away. So many experiences await you. There are cultures to explore, hobbies to take up, people to meet, places to go, dance floors to dance on, fascinating conversations to be had, and people to learn from. There are also individuals who need to learn from you and benefit from you.

Neither your loss nor your divorce define you. Begin actively rebuilding your life and cultivating new interests. Watch for an opportunity and step toward it. If you have children, many of these activities can certainly include them, but find those "alone" moments for yourself as well.

There will be lonely times. I recall one particularly lonely spring-time afternoon. I was walking through an outdoor garden center looking at spring flowers. It was a chilly spring day, and no one was in the garden area but me. Usually this is one of my favorite, brightest times, but at that moment, loneliness overcame me. No one was there to share the flowers of spring with me. The isolation was figuratively and spiritually suffocating.

Sometimes no upbeat advice and no distraction or diversion will give you the comfort you need. Loneliness can crowd in and engulf you like a thick, dark fog so you can no longer see the joy and adventure in your world. This is the time to redesign your thinking.

As I stood in that flower shop, God gave me a powerful insight, a beautiful moment of truth. I realized no matter how lonely this moment was, it was not as lonely as I was when I was married. I've heard many say this same truth. Lonely moments happen when you're on your own, but at least you know you're alone. Nothing feels so lonely as being with someone and being lonely. No isolation is like the emptiness of having an emotionally absent partner.

With that realization I felt at peace, the flowers looked brighter, and my self-pity stopped. The knowledge that being alone and on my own was better than being lonely with someone comforted me. The pity I felt then was for those I've known (myself included), who spent many lonely hours, days, and years in an impossible relationship. I bought myself more flowers that day. In that transformational moment, I learned the simple comfort of taking a deep breath and finding the truth. I hope you will experience your own moment of truth.

Loneliness during and after divorce is very real. As strong as that loneliness is, you can manage it. It is up to you to convert your loneliness into relationship and purpose. Make a plan to deal with your loneliness. Are you alone, or are you befriended by the Spirit of God? God longs to be your most intimate and personal friend and He is always one prayer away.

When my children were small and frightened by a thunderstorm, I responded, "God knows where we are." In the thunderstorm of my life, I frequently have told myself that same truth.

REDESIGNING YOU

Many people in this world would love to create your life's agenda. With the best of intentions they think they know what you need to do. During this time you may have to fight to discover who you really are and not live by others' expectations. I think E. E. Cummings said it best: "To be nobody but yourself in a world which is doing its best night and day to make you everybody else means to fight the hardest battle which any human being can fight and never stop fighting."[3]

UNREASONABLE VOICES

Be mindful of how you talk to yourself—how you encourage or discourage yourself. Self-talk will either get you through this crisis or stop you in your tracks. Don't allow negative self-talk to let you miss out on your party of life.

In comparing your personal self-talk to what others might be thinking, consider this: most often your own self-talk is full of emotion, while other people's thoughts toward you are more objective. Try to keep your self-talk neutral and objective. Don't panic. Consider saying, "I am here, and I refuse to be self-conscious. I will step out of my ego and insecurities and move forward." Appreciate the moment. Be in the present. Don't focus on being alone; focus on what's happening in the world surrounding you. Live life! Chances are very good that those around you are too caught up in their own situations to dwell on yours. Self-obsession is part of the transformation experience. Once you learn that people are not paying attention to your "stuff" like you think they are, you can breathe deep and step forward.

FINDING INTERESTING FACES

If you yearn for more interesting people and events in your life, you need to be open to the company of interesting people. It begins with exposing yourself to places where interesting people hang out. As I mentioned earlier, the theater, bookstores, nice restaurants, art galleries, or libraries might be a good start. Step out of your comfort zone and take the risk to be around different people. Make a true effort to meet and learn from others.

If you are a student of human interaction, watch how people interact and see what you can learn from them. But you must also determine that this is a time to search out places and people and not the next potential date. The dynamics change when people are looking for the next date. Seek experiences first. You will find that other people's experiences will encourage you to create your own interesting experiences. Observe and listen more than you speak. Ask people about their opinions on interesting topics. Interview people you most admire.

THE ART OF CONVERSATION

If you want to truly redesign yourself, communication skills are the perfect place to start. True transformation comes when we look inside of ourselves and honestly review our inward motivations and the hurts that affect our outward actions. How you communicate reveals a lot about you, and it is an improvable skill. Good conversation skills are an art. Like singing and painting, all of us can do it but few of us do it well. Start paying more attention to your conversation. Even in the midst of grieving and hurting, listening to another person can be a respite.

A true conversation is the volleying back and forth of ideas, attention, and honor. Ask questions to further the discussion. Hold back on revealing your own story until the other person completes theirs. Focus on the other person. When you do speak, ask questions that go deeper than surface conversations, beyond topics such as the weather, work, or gossip. Look for interesting subjects to raise such as current events, literature you've read, spiritual questions, and philosophical ideas. Reach past the mundane and excessive details that add nothing to the conversation. Find something stimulating to discuss that adds value and growth to your life and to the person with whom you are speaking.

REDESIGN YOUR LISTENING SKILLS

Just as you redesign your conversation skills, you can reframe your listening skills. Good listeners nurture your soul. They ask a lot of questions because they truly want to hear what other people think. They search for depth. If you want to get to the core of who a person truly is, you have to listen. Good listening involves paying attention to the things that aren't being said. It's making an authentic connection with another human being. It's accepting who they are without judgment or condition. Listen to your next conversation and ask yourself if you sound like someone you would like to be around or would consider good company.

Being in the presence of a good listener is so invigorating! I have a few friends who are wonderful listeners. I love them and need them in my life. My great listening friends are not distracted. They are disciplined to ignore or turn off their phones, texts, and any other possible disruption and remain in the moment. They never rush me. They ask questions and listen intently. I have other friends too who may want to be good listeners, but jump in with their own stories and quickly divert the conversation to themselves. The differences between these two groups of people are subtle forms of communication. I love them both, but great listeners feed and nurture my soul. I want to nurture souls, don't you? You honor people by listening to them. You'll be amazed by what you learn about others and the influence you become. You'll endear yourself to others, and you'll feel good about yourself.

SINGLE THOUGHTS

- Do you say "I" consistently in your conversations?
- What was your last conversation topic? What do you remember most about it?
- Do you really listen to the other person in a conversation, or do you listen in order to respond?
- How can you get to know another person's values, concerns, and passions?
- Do you get bogged down with details that aren't necessary and don't relate to their lives?

SINGLE PERSONALITY

What would you say is your most dominant personality trait? Is it being kind, volatile, laid back, witty, serious, clingy, loud, or cynical? Are you funny, somber, intellectual, or gullible? Are you the humorist or the satirist? Are you "so nice" or primarily a pessimist? Being aware of your dominant personality style will help pinpoint your strengths and reveal how this strength can become a weakness when it's too much. Ask trusted friends what your dominant personality trait is, and be prepared for their honest answers. Understanding your personality strengths and weaknesses allows you to better understand yourself and where you want to grow.

SINGLE THOUGHTS

- How will your dominant personality trait help you in your single life?
- How might it be a disadvantage?
- If you could strengthen one thing about yourself, what would it be?

REDESIGNING YOUR PHYSICAL SELF

In crisis times we need to take good care of ourselves. When things are out of sync it's easy to neglect ourselves. A commitment to nurture your body and get in touch with your physical self requires a conscious choice. Make a VOW to take better care of your body:

V = Vitamins (healthy eating patterns, nutrition awareness)
O = Outlets (laughter, good friends, intellectual stimulation)
W = Walks (exercise and active movement)

Yvonne lost thirty pounds due to the stress of divorce. She decided she liked her new body and determined to keep the weight off by having a positive attitude and living a healthy lifestyle. She got to a place where she could laugh at how she leveraged the crisis to her benefit! And she laughed more because her husband always wanted her to lose the weight. But this time she was doing it for herself and for her own reasons.

TRANSFORMATIONS AND NEW PHASES

Following my divorce twenty years ago, I thought my world had ended, when actually, it had only begun a new and different phase. The negative in your life can be transformed into the positive. It will require taking risks. In so many ways, the last twenty years have been the best years of my life. I love my independence and my reliance upon God, who meets my needs and blesses my life way beyond what I deserve. I've met people who I never would have known had I not become single. You too can turn negative situations into truly positive and wonderful experiences if you venture out. Instead of criticizing or judging yourself, accept your failures. Look at your unsuccessful attempts objectively with a non-condemning attitude.

Say "I can" rather than "I can't and won't try." Say "Never tried it before, but I'll give it a shot!" rather than "Never did it before and it's too late to start now!" Call yourself "honey" (or some other term of endearment) when you talk to yourself. I tend to be too hard on myself, so when I make a wrong turn, miss a deadline, or do something that wasn't the best choice, I'll say "Oh, honey" compassionately. It's not that I don't continue to strive for excellence; I do. I just use this encouraging self-talk to stop demanding perfection from myself or beating myself up.

When new ideas and opportunities come into your life, notice your initial reaction. Take a moment to identify and state your exact feelings, and try to understand any fear or memories the moment conjures up. Then proceed to encourage yourself.

If you trip up, give yourself a break, take the lesson, and move on. Instead of beating yourself up, react with something encouraging and humorous such as:

- "It was a brilliant failure, don't you think?"
- "Didn't I totally discover the way it would *not* work?"
- "Whew! Glad that's over!"
- "I'll give myself an A for effort."

Give yourself grace when you blow it. Look at the big picture. What will it matter in a hundred years or even next week? Chances are, the mistake can be fixed. Nobody could possibly be as hard on you as you are on yourself. Take a deep breath, smile, and give yourself that break. What you achieve or fail to achieve directly relates to how you perceive yourself and your capabilities. Your self-talk shapes your self-perceptions. Encourage yourself whenever you hit a snag.

You are well on your way to your new life. You can do this, and you can do it well. God is the God of second chances. Give the Holy Spirit access to every part of your life and your story. Watch Him create beauty from the ashes of brokenness you give to Him. I've seen hundreds of people years after being divorced. I've witnessed it over and over—people healed who found purpose in service to others. They leveraged the pain they went through into something great. You're embarking on an exciting solo life. Embrace it by accepting your whole self, designing your life to make it a great story.

SINGLE THOUGHTS

- Where do you want to go from here, and what is the first step you need to take?
- Identify one lesson you learned from a situation that initially appeared to be a failure.
- What encouraging self-talk phrase will you use to encourage yourself when you most need that support?

DANCE WITH YOUR SHADOW

His past followed him around as faithfully as his shadow.

Courtney Milan

Alicia and Darren had a third party in their marriage—his mother, who was supporting the family and complicating their marriage. Darren was depressed, he would not get help, and he would not go to work. His mother thought Alicia was awful to leave and take the four children away from their father. It all tormented Alicia. The conditions were unbearable. He forced the children to sit for hours at the table and read their Bible. He scolded them and threatened them with the wrath of God. He shouted at Alicia and said she was a sinner against God for leaving.

Darren's mother thought since she funded the family, she should have a say in family matters. In this, Darren had a shadow he could not stand up against, and it was ruining his present and future. His mother's domination from his past carried over into his adult life and marriage. Her influence and say in the marriage was far from healthy. Darren couldn't see it.

How much of our family history impacts our lives, yet remains unrecognized by us and has more influence than we realize? Some of our family history may be unhealthy for us and our relationships.

The past is the gatekeeper of our belief system. Our beliefs influence how we filter and view the world. We must reckon with this value system and bring peace to it. If your past was hurtful, you might be angry with it or even afraid of it. But since it has already been your partner all of your life, make sure you have learned to dance (accept and lead) with it.

As you stand in your everyday life, you have a shadow that follows you wherever you go. No matter how hard you try to deny it, avoid it, or run away from it, you have this shadow. Sometimes it is evident, at other times obscure, but it is always there. The shadow is your past.

WHAT IT MEANS TO DANCE WITH YOUR SHADOW

Dancing with your shadow means recognizing your past as unchangeable, and understanding how that history has affected the rhythm of your life. Your past doesn't have to dominate your life; you need to lead the dance.

There are several ways you can deal with the shadow of your past:

- You can wrestle with it. This can make you volatile because you never know when it is going to

take hold of you and pin you down. Darren may have wrestled with his past, but Mama won.

- You can despise it. You can allow yourself to become bitter and angry over what happened to you, and you can stay that way. I wonder if Darren's depression had something to do with his sense of hopelessness and lack of control in his own life.

- You can resign yourself to it. You can pretend you are the product of your past and there's nothing you can do about it. Darren allowed his mother to dictate in an unhealthy way and resigned himself to her control.

- You can learn from it. You can blend your past with your present and use it as a forum for learning about yourself and moving on. This would benefit Darren if he could separate himself from his mother, recognize his unhealthy relationship with her, and learn his need for healthy boundaries.

- You can liberate yourself from it. You can design the future so your past becomes a part of your story, a story God is using to unfold your amazing future. This would be the greatest gift Darren could give himself and his family—give this over to God, become a man in control to love his family with strength, and teach others how to create boundaries for family members.

Are you aware of how your past affects your attitude, self-esteem, and relationships today? Think about your past. Think of words spoken and actions taken that influenced your concept of who you are and how you fit into your world. Then choose how you will dance with your own shadow.

MEETING YOUR SHADOW

After my divorce, I considered myself an emotionally healthy person who had come to terms with who and where I was in my life. I felt I was functioning well and had no real relationship issues. I dated a very nice man for a while, had several close friends, and my kids and I had a great relationship. It appeared I was functioning very well until I decided it would be insightful to see a counselor.

Within a few sessions, I began to realize I was indeed an amazing mess! Where had all this stuff come from that had made me who I was (without my permission)? I became a bit anxious about what else lurked below the surface. The crucial question for me was: How is my past affecting me today? If I didn't understand and come to terms with my old baggage, would it sabotage my future relationships and how I relate to my world? How we act in relationships is based on our past core beliefs about ourselves, others, and even God. If some of our beliefs are skewed and invalid, then our view of the world is skewed and invalid. Consequently, we build our world with faulty thinking and imperfect points of reference.

VOICE OF THE PAST

It began in a class in church. As we were discussing a topic I felt strongly about, I contributed several statements, and others did as well.

The service began after class. As I entered the sanctuary, feelings of shame that I had been too outspoken in the class overwhelmed me. Why did I always have to open my mouth? I should have just listened to learn; I should have sat down and shut up! After sitting with tears in my eyes, an affirming thought touched my mind and profoundly warmed heart: "The condemning voice you hear is not the voice of your heavenly Father; it is the voice of your earthly father." The statement surprised me by its contrast to what I was feeling, and a genuine feeling of calm replaced the shame. I sat there amazed at the sudden clarity of that profound truth right when my past collided with my present.

During my childhood, I had heard the negative, frightening voice of my father. So many times, even as an adult, his voice influenced my thoughts and my self-talk. That voice of my earthly father was oppressive, judgmental, and accusatory. That morning in church, the glorious, overriding voice of my ultimate Father awakened me to find freedom from that unhealthy, demanding voice. In contrast to my earthly father, God's gentle Spirit showed amazing love and was approachable and comforting. His Spirit was encouraging and uplifting, and possessed a gentleness I will never forget. And the most profound truth was that He was on my side. That day I found comfort I had never known before and felt accepted in a way I never had before. I gained great comfort in verses from Isaiah, because it identifies the same Spirit that met me that morning:

> *I, even I, am the one who wipes out your transgressions*
> *for My own sake, and I will not remember your sins.*
> *Put Me in remembrance; let us argue our case together.*
> *State your cause, that you may be proved right.*
>
> Isaiah 43:25–26 NASB

That morning I felt God's Spirit come alongside of me and be the ultimate judge and comforter at the same time. He proved to be my ally, my defender. I felt Him stand up against the wrong of my past and redeem it. It was personal and profound. Maybe this intimate moment was when I realized my true adoption where I could cry, "Abba, Father" just like the verse says:

> *The Spirit you received does not make you slaves, so that you live*
> *in fear again; rather, the Spirit you received brought about your*
> *adoption to sonship. And by him we cry, "Abba, Father."*
>
> Romans 8:15

FACING YOUR PAST

My father died when I was thirteen. And I was in my midthirties when I sat in that church pew. The shadow of his disapproval followed me and influenced me all of those years. You might have a similar story stemming from your childhood, whether the voices you heard were right or wrong, supportive or oppressive. These are your shadows. The question is, what do you do with them? How do you stop listening to invalid voices from the past so you don't sabotage yourself and future relationships? Only by conscientiously and intentionally replacing them with a new voice, a real voice of reason, truth, and encouragement, will you find peace.

I am only now beginning to grasp that losing my father at such an early age had a lasting influence on me. I had so little time to understand my father and all his struggles or to build a relationship. My early loss raises many questions that to connect with themes throughout my life: Did my father's early death inadvertently and wrongly teach me the lesson that men can't be trusted and they always leave? Did I grow up believing men are emotionally distant and unable to fully love; therefore, I should never be vulnerable? Was my inability to let myself fully trust and love my defense against potential loss?

Search your own history for shadows that may have influenced your assumptions about yourself, life, and relationships. I encourage you to spend some time reflecting and working on this highly important but often overlooked aspect of your life. What early experiences may have cast a shadow over your childhood? And have you come to terms with them as an adult?

Begin by searching your life to understand the narrative from your past and then hold it up to the light of Scripture. Find out what you've absorbed that is contrary to Scripture, and replace it with the sure knowledge you are under Christ's lordship. You are a child of the Father. Let go of false ideas so you can move forward with your life.

FACE IT

Discern the old messages still influencing your life. They are not always obvious, and understanding them requires time, prayer, and patience. One way to see their effect on your life is to examine your attitudes, values, and self-talk. Are they positive, encouraging, and hopeful, or condemning, shaming, and looking for perfectionism?

What were you taught about finances, food, work ethic, the value of women, and appropriate attitudes toward men and children? Were those teachings contrary to the Word of God? Were they helpful or oppressive? Take a few moments and write them down in detail. What from your past continues to influence your thought processes now and, consequently, affects your life and relationships? With focus and time, you can do this on your own, though if you need to work with a counselor for a while, I highly recommend it.

We probably all suffer from our own version of negative, oppressive words from our pasts, the kind that tell us to "sit down and shut up." By recognizing past unhealthy voices and their stifling influence, we can learn to recognize and turn away from those messages. We can block out those that tell us to be less than what we are in Jesus Christ. The more aware we become of our own shadows, the easier it will be to recognize them in other people's attitudes and behaviors. We can learn how to identify the old, wrong voices in our head (like prejudices and attitudes we were told and shown as a child) and take control of our reactions, understanding we don't have to submit to these voices or react in anger once we recognize them. We can use a different point of reference to determine our reactions. Replace those voices of the past with a greater, healthier voice of authority, and react to this greater voice. For me, the greatest voice is the voice of God through the Scriptures. Scriptures are powerful when you claim them and internalize them.

We begin to live powerfully as we examine and discern which false teachings we have received. Again, these could be core values related to the value of yourself, the value of children, the display of affection, the value and respect of other people (specific people or people in general), or a multitude of others. Then we put those on the cross and claim a greater heritage for our children and ourselves. This is what new birth is all about and how God wishes to cleanse us from our past and its influences—the influence of our parents' sins and our own.

SINGLE THOUGHTS

- What favorite childhood experiences or positive teachings have helped you as an adult?
- How have early hurts or disappointments marked your attitude, and how willing are you to talk about these experiences?
- Is there an area of your past that is too difficult to face or you feel you need to keep hidden? What is it, and do you need to heal from it?
- What early decisions and assumptions have you made that may have put limits on your relationships?

LOUD VOICES, DARK SHADOWS

You may have wondered what you do with the darkest shadows, such as abuse, trauma, or shameful teachings of your past. Sometimes you can't disown them on your own, nor should you. You may think because these events happened so many years ago they can't affect you today, but they do. I found in my own experience that by dealing with my issues instead of hiding them, I gained a clearer perspective on my life. In being willing to deal with the shadows of my past, I can think and move through life more freely and clearly, and the shadows don't cloud my thinking as they once did.

You too can let go of those manipulating voices. Understanding and acknowledging their presence helps bring everything into the open, so you can understand their hold on you. From there you can take control of, keep control of, and eventually dance with your shadow in celebration and appreciation of your rich history, good and bad, that makes you the unique and wonderful individual you are.

We know intimacy is foundational for a healthy relationship. Yet sometimes we build protective walls to shield us from the bad, not realizing we're also blocking out the good. Dr. Dean Ornish says, "The heart develops a particularly strong armor to protect and defend itself, but the same emotional defenses that protect us can also isolate us if they always remain up. We can only be intimate to the degree that we are willing to be open and vulnerable."[1]

Intimacy requires transparency. Sometimes we tuck away parts of ourselves, and we don't realize they are hidden. And we don't know how to get beyond our past. We yearn to be known and accepted and loved for who we are, but we get in the way of that ideal. So we must be transparent with ourselves. We may cling to our old defenses to shield ourselves against further hurt because they are familiar, even if they are ineffective. How quickly we can once again become that small child full of shame if our past was shame-based. We have to face our history honestly and courageously, and then appreciate it for the place it has in our lives.

Melinda, a divorce support group member, modeled this well. She decided she needed further counseling to move beyond her history of bad relationships. Why did she continually find the wrong men who personified her abusive father? Similarly, you may feel it is time to face some hidden truths in your life through counseling or some other space that allows you to be vulnerable and honest.

Dealing with the hard things of our pasts can be tough and uncomfortable. Yet, remarkably, we are dealing with our pasts every day anyway, because we are living out the same attitudes and lifestyles. You can take the lead or be led by it. You will naturally follow the path you have been taught until you intercede to change it. Open up your entire self to healing; learn to deal with the parts of you that limit your potential and relationships. Take the step toward controlling your shadow rather than allowing it to control you. You choose the music and you name the dance.

THE DANCE IS ALSO A BATTLE

Replaying old tapes, voices, and actions holds us back and makes us feel defeated. We believe lies, stay stuck, and never become all we are meant to be. "Sit down and shut up!" played on repeat in Kathryn's head ever since she was a small child. It is no wonder she remained abnormally introverted and unable to speak up for herself. No wonder a dominant man stepped into her father's place and kept her in that corner, becoming more and more abusive until she sought safety in a shelter and support from a divorce group.

God tells us to protect ourselves, to put on the whole armor of God.

> Finally, be strong in the Lord and in the strength of his might. Put on the whole armor of God, that you may be able to stand against the schemes of the devil. For we do not wrestle against flesh and blood, but against the rulers, against the authorities, against the cosmic powers over this present darkness, against the spiritual forces of evil in the heavenly places.... In all circumstances take up the shield of faith, with which you can extinguish all the flaming darts of the evil one; and take the helmet of salvation, and the sword of the Spirit, which is the word of God, praying at all times in the Spirit, with all prayer and supplication. (Eph. 6:10–12, 16–18 ESV)

The sword of the Word, the shield of faith, the belief God is for you and not against you—strengthens you as you hold onto this truth: God longs for you to be healthy and objective about your past, remembering only the lessons and His power overcoming all sin. And it is never God's will for you to stay stuck, to feel defeated, or to live in the shame of your past. He placed all of your defeat upon Christ. That is the beauty of the cross.

VIBRATIONS OF CHILDHOOD

I asked a psychotherapy professor at a dinner one night if we ever truly get over our childhood. He put his hands on the table and shook it gently. He said childhood is like an ever-present vibration; for some of us it vibrates gently, but for others it shakes violently. And while every possible variation in between those two extremes may occur, to some extent, the vibration is always there. If what he said is true, how can we possibly ignore the effects our pasts have upon us, and how can they not influence the way we relate to the world and our relationships with others?

Another illustration of the long-lasting impact of childhood experiences comes to mind. Dr. Jane Helmstead, who specializes in childhood attachment disorders, states it this way:

> Attachment develops through the sensitive and nurturing responses of a loving caregiver. The child feels protected and gets his needs met. Children thus develop a trusting relationship towards the caregiver and empathic feelings towards those around them. These positive experiences become the foundation for healthy relationships in the future. Attachment disorders, however, develop from a lack of social and emotional support, and

often present due to abuse or neglect at the hands of a primary caregiver. The child's needs go unmet and he becomes insecure, anxious or avoidant of any opportunity to attach to others.[2]

It's hard to fathom that babies push away what they want and need so much. It's equally hard to comprehend the lifelong impact of those early months of life. But even as adults we hunger for our needs to be met and our wounds to be healed. We hunger to be attached to those who will meet our needs. But like the children who suffered without healthy attachment, we struggle to know how to get our current deepest needs met because we don't understand our past unmet needs and the hurts that darken our lives.

The past can be stubborn. Licensed counselor Beth Bolthouse explains this well:

> Even after we have worked through the negative issues of our past, those issues can rear their ugly head again. When something traumatic occurs in the present it can connect with an old wound of the past. Even if that wound has healed, the past tries to re-engage with the 'old tapes' of negative thinking, shame, blame, unforgiveness, and anger—whatever it is that we have struggled with and worked through. Ask the Holy Spirit to remind you to focus on the truth, so the present wound is able to be grieved in a healthy way to disconnect from the past. The promises of God are powerful in this process![3]

WHOM WE CHOOSE

Psychologists agree that in our intimate relationships, we unknowingly choose an image of our parents, even if it is unhealthy. In my life, my relationship with my father and my relationship with my husband were shadows I had to recognize and come to terms with. Only then was I able to dance with that part of my history. As a result, I began experiencing healthier, more equal relationships. Slowly, I learned not all men wanted to leave me, use negative energy against me, squelch me, control me, or want me to sit down and shut up. I discovered some of them were healthy and mature enough to want to know and love me. I've found not all men mirror the images of my past.

IS THERE AN INNOCENT PARTY?

I've concluded that even though I was not the one to end my marriage, several of the marriage issues were mine. Perhaps I shut down and waited for my husband to leave. In fact, maybe I expected him to leave because he was unhappy with me and like my emotionally distant father. In choosing him, had I set myself up for a familiar situation with a man who would always be emotionally unavailable? I shut down emotionally during my marriage just as I had in my childhood. I did it to protect myself.

Risking an honest look at my role and my reactions gave me power over my past. Owning our parts, without excuses or rationalizations, gives us freedom. Then once we understand our roles, we ask forgiveness of God and forgive ourselves. And if my former husband were still living, I would ask him for forgiveness too.

Relationships get complicated and repetitive. If you look closely you can see where and how your past influenced your marriage. You can then determine if that's what you want in your future. You don't have to overanalyze your past, but reflect on its influence so you can add the appropriate light if you need to make the shadow disappear. Otherwise, your next life partner will be the same type of person you've chosen in the past. I'm sure you've heard of the woman who marries the "same man" over and over again. The only difference is the DNA profile.

Dealing with heart wounds takes work, courage, vulnerability, and commitment. Everyone wants healing without cost, but it costs. Consider the consequences if you don't—more unhealthy relationships, more wasted time, life, and focus. We must repeat the mantra "I want healing and I don't care what it takes." The deeper you go, the closer you will find God. He is the Great Physician who heals those wounds created so long ago. He is the salve we need and offers the freedom to move forward. Once freed from our shadows, we are not as prone to be manipulated by our pasts. We lead the dance.

SINGLE THOUGHTS

- In some ways we contributed to the relationship that ended in divorce. How can you lovingly forgive yourself for the part you played?
- What did you see in your spouse that could also have been a trait of someone in your childhood?
- How did you protect yourself when you were little, and are you still using this same self-protection today?

DANCING WITH THE PAST

There she was, the little flower girl on the reception dance floor, dancing all by herself, her arms outstretched, her white dress floating around her as she twirled. Sometimes her hands reached upward as her shoulders and body flowed with the pulse of the music. She seemed to ride on the rhythm. She didn't notice anyone around her. She was just an innocent little girl with a free spirit who just had to dance. The music alone was her companion, and her shadow spilled across the dance floor. She danced with such abandon and freedom.

Don't we all long to enjoy that freedom, especially over our pasts? As we work through our shadows they can become things of beauty and God's grace instead of shame. And in time, we'll see God's hand bringing forth new life: "Forget the former things; do not dwell on the past. See, I am doing a new thing! Now it springs up; do you not perceive it? I am making a way in the wilderness and streams in the wasteland" (Isa. 43:18–19).

Celebrate all of who you are, not in spite of your past but because of it. God will use that past to build you up, never to tear you down. Use it for your good and to give you empathy for others to minister to. What you have overcome is part of what made you the incredible person you are today. Embrace the lessons you've learned as you take your past lightly. The dance will flow and you will take the lead. Dance with your shadow; it has been your partner all of your life.

9

LESSONS FROM THE DATING FIELD

*The time you are most prepared for dating is when
you don't need anyone to complete you, fulfill you,
or instill in you a sense of worth or purpose.*

Myles Munroe

Soon after my divorce, a coworker of mine said, "Well, Kathey, I guess you'll be playing the field now." I responded, "It's been twenty years, and I don't even know where the field is!"

I found the field of dating. It is expansive, diverse, and sometimes mysterious. The field has a few snakes in it, but for the most part, delightful people and wonderful surprises fill it. I never intended to chronicle any of my relationships, nor did I imagine they would provide such rich learning experiences, but indeed they did. I hope my lessons will help prepare you for what you will face in the world of dating. Most of all, I hope they will help raise your awareness of red flags or warning signs indicating unhealed or unhealthy people. The whole point is to avoid making the same mistake over and over again.

I placed this important chapter on dating toward the end of this book for a reason. I'm hoping you won't go there—into the field—until you're truly ready. To be ready is to take care of your old business first.

You'll know you're ready when you've spent the necessary time to grieve, heal, accept where you are, and begin living as a healthy single adult. You have forgiven your former spouse, the kids are taken care of, and your finances are relatively in order. You've established you are a healed person in the process of defining who you are and where you want to go in life. You are redesigning your life with an open spirit to what God wants for you. You've taken care of your old business and have a fuller understanding of your life's purpose. In essence, you are prepared to create a new life for yourself.

SINGLE FEARS

Many people fear being alone. So to make sure they are not they settle for a less-than-suitable relationship. They fantasize the relationship will be the answer to life and happiness. I hope after reading this chapter you will find that being alone is not so terrible and actually has many advantages. It is not something to be feared but embraced. When you get healthy on your own and find you don't need anybody to make you whole, *then* you are ready for the next relationship. Many people never reach that point and marry or enter the next relationship much too soon and live with less than their heart's desire, or more importantly, less than God's desire.

I regret the need for morbidity, but one of our fears is dying alone. If you are like many, you fear you will find yourself on your own bed alone and dying with no one there to hold your hand, pray over you, or encourage you with what heaven will be. That is good reason to develop caring relationships with other people in general and to maintain healthy relationships with your children. Many of us will die alone in car accidents, of heart attacks … Need I go on in my morbid musings? If you are in a relationship, your spouse may be away or the kids may all be busy when a health crisis arises. So instead of fearing dying alone, fear dying without the comfort of knowing God will take you through this final step.

While death is a physical experience, it is also a spiritual one, so allow God to give you peace about it. Maintain your relationship with Him and have the faith to know He will not abandon you or forsake you in that incredible time of need. Relieve this fear by faith, knowing He will be with you when death comes. Only God knows that appointment so prepare for it by living life abundantly. Find comfort in the apostle Paul's words: "For I am convinced that neither death nor life, neither angels nor demons, neither the present nor the future, nor any powers, neither height nor depth, nor anything else in all creation, will be able to separate us from the love of God that is in Christ Jesus our Lord" (Rom. 8:38–39).

Regardless of what I say, I know that in your heart you may want to find your next relationship. As you pursue this relationship, please take these lessons to heart. It's anguishing when people contact me and tell me that a relationship, or worse yet a marriage, was a mistake and they are ending it.

Don't get me wrong; I could share fabulous stories of good marriages after divorce. And I want that for you if you wish to remarry and it's God's plan for you.

My friend Janna, for example, spent fifteen years after her divorce searching for her next relationship. She was convinced remarrying would make her life complete. Her dating life seemed like a revolving door of men throughout those years, until Janna realized she had never fully healed from her divorce. At that time, she hired a life coach and went to work on herself. She gave up her search for the perfect mate and surrendered to the One who would heal her heart for good. She began to fully enjoy her single life. And guess what? Within a year, she met a man who became her best friend and later her husband.

Are you searching for the perfect mate, or are you searching for perfect peace within yourself? Are you seeking to find wholeness for yourself through other people? Don't let fear of being alone drive you in the wrong direction. And don't waste years chasing the elusive perfect relationship. For now, put your energy into healing and postpone the next relationship until you are whole and complete being single.

THE MOST VITAL RELATIONSHIP

I believe we come to understand our value more completely by knowing who we are in God's design rather than establishing the next relationship. Start your new life by finding your strengths and your God-given gifts that lead to your life's goals and dreams. That is the key to your happiness. The only relationship that can fully complete us is the one with our Creator. There is no substitute; yet we sometimes search for what only God can fill in other people. You find your peace by finding God first, through a relationship with His Son, Jesus Christ.

What is that? It is not the practices of religion or rituals in churches, although they can greatly enhance your relationship. I am speaking of searching for your own personal relationship with God. Scripture records God's promise: "Then you will call upon Me and come and pray to Me, and I will listen to you. And you will seek Me and find Me when you search for Me with all your heart" (Jer. 29:12–13 NASB). God honors those searching for Him. He will provide for your needs. I have found Him to be the best husband over the past twenty-one years. He provides tender moments, guiding moments, a fullness to soothe my loneliness, and a purpose as I watch Him work through me. It is a special kind of communion with God when you see God work through you. Witnessing His actions in my life far outweighs watching my own.

SINGLE THOUGHTS

- What healing do you need to do before you consider dating?
- What are some resources you could use to help you heal further?
- How would you describe your relationship with God? Do you trust in Jesus Christ? How can you make your relationship stronger and more personal during this time in your life?

DATING IN THE NEW WORLD

If you are like many, you'll ignore all the words of warning and jump into the next relationship. You'll think you know better and you can handle it. Even deep down you may be thinking, *I can handle this one, God.* And then months or years from now, you'll look back and think, *Wow, God was right. I wish I had taken more time to heal and become a strong individual than to go into a relationship when I wasn't ready. I wish I had started slower.*

A year or so after my divorce, the dust had settled. I had finished my old business and nestled into my singlehood. I soon realized I was responsible for my own life and happiness. No one was going to come to my door and hand me a new life, new opportunities, or a new relationship. So I stepped out into the world of dating.

How intriguing and fascinating people are if you are open to getting to know them. As I dated new people, the world opened up to me in many ways and I expanded my borders and my understanding of the world. Such exploration, with equal measure of guts and precaution, can be exciting. Encounters with new ideas, diverse values, peculiar ideologies, different faiths, various lifestyles, inspiring core values, community leaders, and more thrilled me. But dating can also be exhausting. None of those relationships led to marriage or this book would have a different title. I wearied of the search, effort, and time it took. There are other ways to gain life experiences without dating. In fact, other ways could have offered this excitement and more, like working on building my own network or going after my passions of life in full force. The most valuable experiences to me were the ones that taught me lessons I will never forget. I learned to listen to my gut.

I'm not sure you can go through the dating life and get it right all the time. I made plenty of mistakes and racked up some regrets. But you can learn to recognize red flags and avoid regrets if you move slowly.

DATING DISORDERS

Perhaps there is such a thing as a dating disorder. Beware, lest you fall into one these:

OCD—Obsessive Compulsive Dater—one who spends an exorbitant amount of time and attention on dating. You check the online dating site fifteen times a day. You do this and other things to alleviate obsessive fears and intrusive thoughts you are going to be alone and dateless on Saturday night, in fact on the next three Saturday nights. This behavior disrupts your daily life.

ADD—Attention Deficit Dater—a combination of inattentiveness, distractibility, hyperactivity, and impulsive behavior. You display inattentiveness to your close friends, ignore your own growth and desires, and are distracted by wondering when and where you'll meet your next potential date. You become obsessed and inattentive to life, believing you will become alive when you are in the next relationship. Consider if you are spending too much mental capital on the subject of dating and the next relationship and are wasting the present time and all it has to offer.

CONFESSIONS OF A SERIAL DATER

If those disorders weren't enough, I also have a few confessions to share. I offer them for your serious consideration as you venture into dating and the single life. Since I have been single the last twenty-one years, I've had plenty of opportunities to make some smart decisions along the way—and some not-so-smart decisions. With dating comes the marriage proposals, heartbreak, wishing for a marriage proposal that never happens, dating disasters, and cries of "What was I thinking?" I hope these confessions will help you clarify what you want in your next relationship and save you some time and heartache on your way to finding it.

Confession 1—I wasn't sure what I wanted.

I didn't always know what I was searching for. Vague thinking such as *I'll know it when I see it* or *I'll know him when I see him* wasted my time and theirs. Pray for clarity. As Christian psychologist Georgia Shaffer put it so beautifully, "When you know yourself, you'll be less likely to lose yourself in the next relationship."[1]

I do not want to discourage anyone who truly longs for relationship; however, I encourage you to study the apostle Paul's words seriously: "Now to the unmarried and the widows I say: It is good for them to stay unmarried, as I do" (1 Cor. 7:8). You are better off alone than with the wrong person. Why would Paul encourage us to stay as we are? Does God know more than we do? Could this singleness simplify your life?

Questions later in this chapter will help you assess where you are and what you are looking for. Take the questions to heart—they may save yours.

We want the butterflies in the stomach, the tingles, the goose bumps, the excitement of their calls. It is all wonderful and beautiful. And we will trade a lot searching for these: time, energy, and sometimes morals. But tingles fade and butterflies fly off. Infatuation is not a basis for relationship—not if you are searching for something authentic and real.

I also dated to assure myself I still had it. Not sure what "it" is, but somehow I had to figure out if I still "had it." I'd been rejected so I set out to prove myself. And I did. I was worthy of being loved and attractive enough to get attention. But the flesh never stops. It will never come to a point on its own when it is satisfied and content. Contentment comes from a heart full of the knowledge of who God is in your life and from knowing He longs for relationship with you every single day of your life. And when we find our godly mission, then we can reach true contentment. Then we can come to peace with who we are and settle that we still have "it."

Confession 2—Feelings are not always trustworthy.

Feelings are not only untrustworthy; they can even be dangerous. At times, mine led me astray from heeding important warning signs, such as, this is not the right relationship or it is moving too quickly. But feelings are so powerful, how can they not be trusted? Powerful doesn't mean they are the truth. Feelings alone won't show you deeper things like character or other harsh truths you may need to see. Your mind should control your feelings not the other way around. The Bible says, "The mind governed by the Spirit is life and peace" (Rom. 8:6) and "You will keep in perfect peace those whose minds are steadfast, because they trust in you" (Isa. 26:3). Life becomes complicated so quickly, because people allow their feelings to guide them and throw their senses out the window.

I don't mean to throw cold water on your emotions, but I also don't want you blindsided while in a vulnerable place because you can't see beyond your emotions. When someone tells you how wonderful you are and gives you the much-needed attention you have longed for, be cautious. Feelings are beautiful, and love is the most beautiful feeling of all. However, truth floats. It will not be kept submerged under feelings for too long. Give a new relationship at least eighteen months before you really give serious consideration to your feelings.

Confession 3—I wasted a lot of time.

I could have had my PhD by now or become a nuclear physicist (except for the fact I'm terrible in math). The whole world was open to me! Did I really have the time to spend pursuing a relationship? That longing inside me was deep and real. But not all the people I found were deep or real. I wasted time with people who were not the best choices for me. If I had known myself more definitively and been focused on what was worthwhile, I would have been further ahead today. I would have been further ahead in education, writing plays, performing, speaking, training, and making memories with the right people—for me, my children, and my grandchildren.

The best relationships bring out the best in you. If they don't bring out your best or if they sacrifice your values, they are wasting your time. So consider—what do you tolerate in a relationship? Do your relationships reflect your values?

What could you do better with your time? Develop yourself, your ministry, your leadership skills, or your gift of painting flowerpots! I could have found earlier what purpose God had for me—to serve other people and grow into the best possible me. I understand how real and strong loneliness can be. We will always need human relationships, but not all human relationships are the best use of our time and the best for us.

I say this to you for you to consider. Weigh it in your own life, and pursue whatever your heart and God leads. But see the beauty of accepting the side of the fence you are on now. I was stronger than I realized, and you are too. Further your education, write a book, teach a group, and take the lead in your own life.

Confession 4—Rejection is a weird way to find your direction.

I was sitting at my computer a couple days after a first date. My date emailed that he decided the drive was a little long and he was pursuing a relationship with someone else. *Hmmm,* I thought, *I have been "deselected."* It wouldn't be the last time. Dating can be more complex at this stage of life. If someone doesn't like you, it may be a gift and a time saver. Mosey on down the road so you can find someone who does like you. Do not apologize for who you are. (Unless you're a jerk, in which case you need to do some self-examination.) Let people reject you—it's good for you! Rejection allows you to eliminate one path in life, and there are possibly thousands of better paths.

The beautiful thing about rejection is there are no games being played and no time being wasted. "The truth will set you free" (John

8:32). Even the hard truth will. Truth, no matter how painful, rescues us. See people for who they really are. See the truth not what you want the truth to be or what you can create the truth to be. Better things await down the road; just keep walking.

Confession 5—I spurned the greatest Lover.

While I was out pursuing relationships and human love, I was being pursued by the deepest love. Did you know God pursues you? The Lord longs to be as intimate as a lover, the one who loves you with the ultimate love and sacrifice. Many verses in Scripture show our relationship with God through Christ being one of joy, intimacy, and pleasure. The psalmist declared, "You make known to me the path of life; in your presence there is fullness of joy; at your right hand are pleasures forevermore" (Ps. 16:11 ESV).

God also compares the love in marriage to how He will rejoice over you. You will be His delight: "As the bridegroom rejoices over the bride, so shall your God rejoice over you" (Isa. 62:5 ESV). Trust this verse and concept and watch for how it is revealed in your life.

In the book of Hosea, God's describes His love for His wayward children. God instructs Hosea to pick a wayward wife to illustrate how His people are unfaithful to Him. He continues to love us, yet we prostitute ourselves for cheap lovers. Hosea speaks of the Lord's love for His unfaithful chosen nation Israel: "But then I will win her back once again. I will lead her into the desert and speak tenderly to her there" (Hosea 2:14 NLT).

God's love is more precious than any, because He *is* love. This One, who drew me close at night and caressed my heart with love in the world around me, watched me fall asleep every evening. I ignored Him many times. But He was always there waiting, anticipating when and if I would call to Him. I went to other lovers; I settled for cheap imitations. The true Lover of my soul patiently waited. For years—for decades—He waited. Who does that? Why would He not give up?

Why wait for marriage, the symbol of Christ and the church, when you can have Christ Himself? God is closer to us than we think. Psalm 139 tells us He knows us, every hair on our head, and still loves us. I want that kind of lover! My heart echoes the psalmist's words: "How precious are your thoughts about me, O God. They cannot be numbered! I can't even count them; they outnumber the grains of sand! And when I wake up, you are still with me!" (Ps. 139:17–18 NLT). Have you ever had a lover who wasn't with you when the morning came? God remains in the morning and through the night and in sickness and in health. He promises, "Then you will know that I am the LORD; those who hope in me will not be disappointed" (Isa. 49:23).

God is personal and close in His love for us: "For the LORD your God is living among you. He is a mighty savior. He will take delight in you with gladness. With his love, he will calm all your fears. He will rejoice over you with joyful songs" (Zeph. 3:17 NLT).

This puts a whole new perspective on the single life doesn't it? This love changes you. The world looks different, priorities change, and faith becomes your new love language. God's love makes you long for something more than flesh can deliver. His sensitivity to your soul gives you sensitivity to the souls of others. Maybe what you seek in your dating relationship is God's love and presence, being loved by Him for who you are, treasured and adored. He is the "someone" who would sacrifice for you and prove His love for you. He did, He does, and He continues to do so.

MAKING MEMORIES

God doesn't have the formula for love and life wrong. Search for God first and the rest will follow.

> *Seek ye first the kingdom of God, and his righteousness,*
> *and all these things shall be added unto you.*
>
> Matthew 6:33 KJV

The formula for starting your next relationship is:

- Be honest—honest with others and honest with yourself.
- Seek God's will—God knows what will make you happy before you do. Seek Him and you might be surprised at how rich and fulfilling His will is.
- Listen to God's voice—God longs to talk to you about your relationships. Ignore Him at your own peril.

What if the best thing for you is not another marriage? What if you discover richness in His plan for you being single? What happens if you redirect time, energy, and thought to your purpose in life and to those to whom you were meant to minister and contribute?

SINGLE THOUGHTS

- Do you ignore red flags because you want to be "with someone" so badly?
- Make a list of what you are looking for.
- Where should you find relationship?
- What boundaries are necessary for you in a healthy relationship?
- What does God want for you in a relationship? Is it time you asked Him? Is it possible He wants more for you than you are currently willing to accept?
- Can you learn to be stubbornly dependent upon God to meet all your needs?
- What are trust and faith? Can you really trust God with your life?

GOD KNOWS WHAT IS BEST FOR YOU

You'll get it right; learn from your mistakes and mine. Take your time—pay attention to those red flags of warning. Listen to your gut and the Spirit of God. He will save you years of heartache.

I listened intently one Sunday to the pastor teach about what a marriage is designed to be. He spoke of the man's role of sacrifice for the wife and family. He spoke beautifully, clearly, and with biblical authority on the role, using Scriptures and Christ's life as examples. I was in a relationship, one I thought I was going to be in forever. As I left the church that Sunday, I heard God's voice say to me, *He will never sacrifice for you.* I knew it was God because it contradicted the way my mind was thinking at the time. And the voice lined up with Scripture (always a litmus test), and it responded to and aligned with what I knew was true in my spirit. It was hard to hear, but time proved it to be correct.

You can only hide the truth or rationalize it away for so long. Save yourself time and heartache and listen to the Spirit early. He's smarter than we give Him credit for. God was right; this man never would have sacrificed for me in a godly way. God is always right.

The necessity of following God's wisdom always applies to our actions within our relationships. At one point I was offending God in my relationship and heard a pastor speak on the sacredness of intimate relationships. I felt very convicted. I grieved, and I realized I was missing out on God and His blessing because I was living out of His will. After church, still feeling guilty, I sat at a restaurant with the man I was dating and a friend. Our seats were in a spacious area with several windows, overlooking a beautiful lake. I don't know whether to chuckle or cry when I think about it now, but suddenly, a bird, some crazy, little, God-directed bird flew through an open window and smacked the side of my head. I was stunned. *Okay, God, I get Your message. I'm done for good. No physical relationships until I enter marriage.*

Since that decision, God has blessed my life in numerous ways that reassure me absolutely nothing can or will replace what God wants to bless me with. So listen to His Word; it offers protection, guidance, and blessings beyond your imagination when you fully follow Him. I have learned over the years to trust Him with absolutely everything—money, sex, relationships, connections, successes—all of it. He has higher plans than you or I do.

Note the importance of being under the teaching of God's Word. Don't think for a moment God wants to deny you happiness or success or close relationships. Quite the opposite is true. He wants what is best for you, and He knows what is best for you. He wants better than what any physical relationship or "butterflies" can give you.

DATING IS DIFFERENT THE SECOND TIME AROUND

People bring lessons with them when they come into your life. It doesn't matter how old you are or how experienced you've become, you can learn a lot about yourself in your relationships, even the wrong ones. My new relationships, even those that were short-lived, helped me clarify what I wanted, what I did not want, and what was unacceptable.

When we were young and naive, we didn't realize the complexity of relationships. Things are simpler, and sometimes superficial. As adults we need to consider the details of someone's past. Are they healed? Are they angry in life? Are they in a hurry to create a relationship? What are they looking for? Do they need rescuing, or are they looking for someone to rescue? Do they need to prove themselves? Observe carefully, listen intently, and read between the lines. That's one of the things your gut can do best if you let it. Too many times I have heard in my divorce groups from those who saw the red flags, then ignored them—to their detriment.

Some of us form emotional attachments fast. Safeguard your heart until the person earns your trust. Proceed with caution, regardless of the pretty flowers, soft words, impeccable manners, or good looks. Step back. Take a realistic look at what you want and need in a relationship. Don't try to force the fit. Don't feel as if this is your last chance at a relationship because that's just not true.

SINGLE THOUGHTS

- If you were to write a profile on yourself for online dating, what would you write?
- What core traits are you looking for in a partner?
- Define what comprises a healthy, authentic relationship for you.

DETHRONING THE QUEEN (OR KING) OF RATIONALIZATION

Oh, the amazing ways we deceive ourselves into believing what we want to be true. We deny reality and try to fit what doesn't fit. We want to have life the way we want it, rather than seeing and accepting it the way it is. Trying to create what isn't there, we become the "queen (or king) of rationalization." We think we have the power to create our own reality. Not only do we rationalize our own actions and thoughts, but we also rationalize the actions and thoughts of others. It is a dangerous imaginary land. The truth surfaces after you have wasted time and your heart is deeply connected with another. Rationalization doesn't work in everyday life, and it certainly doesn't work in relationships. Don't rationalize; allow time to know the truth and then act on the truth as quickly as possible. The day of reckoning will come, but the later this happens the more painful and difficult it becomes.

SIMPLY REVEALING

It's important to act on a red flag when you sense one and to know the heart of a person with whom you are in relationship. After I dated a man for nearly a year, I sensed something was lacking but I couldn't put my finger on it. I asked him to write a paragraph about our relationship. I wanted to know what he thought about our relationship and how he defined it. Since he was a highly educated man, this should have been an easy request. But he refused to do it. Actually, he couldn't do it because he didn't feel the depth in the relationship I did.

I wasn't testing him as much as seeking an indicator of where the man's heart was, and I got what I asked for. This red flag and my response to it taught me something crucial: if you don't have his heart, you don't *have* him, and if you don't have his heart, no matter what else he has to offer, you don't *want* him. Why? Because you can't keep someone who isn't all in. It's only a matter of time before some shiny object will carry this person away.

I also used what I call the "breakfast table test." I asked myself these questions: Is this the person I could sit across from at the breakfast table every day—with me in my rawest form (before coffee) and he in his rawest form? Could I do that for the rest of my life? For me, these revealing questions clarified and answered a lot. I'm not into a relationship for show. I want it real or not at all.

LESSONS LEARNED (WHAT TO WATCH FOR)

1. Intensity doesn't mean authenticity. Physical attraction can lead you to believe there is really something there of substance or authenticity. Is it lust or love? It takes time for a relationship to prove its authenticity. Intensity wanes with time; authenticity grows.

2. The negatives are often positives in disguise. The relationships that didn't work out freed me to seek a better relationship. If you are the one turned down, you are free to move on, to discover more of who you are, and to head where you need to be in your life.

3. Insecurities cannot be the glue that holds a relationship together. This reality poses a strong argument for going through your healing process so you can become stronger and healthier for yourself and the person you are dating. When you become strong and independent, you attract like-minded people with greater potential for creating strong relationships rather than those with unhealthy dependencies.

4. You must be yourself, even if it means ending a relationship. Refuse to settle for less than what you dream of or deserve. Do not compromise who you are or what you believe is right for a relationship. No person or relationship is worth the cost. Being alone is a better choice than losing yourself in a superficial relationship that is a figment of your imagination and will eventually implode.

5. He may be more in love with the idea of having someone than he is in love with you. Sometimes the relationship wasn't about me at all. It was about his life, insecurities, needing to have someone with him, or proving himself as a man. Some men and women need to

validate their worth by seeing themselves through another person's eyes. If you see this red flag, move on because it devalues you.

6. Beware of fresh wounds (in the very recently single). This may even include you at this time if you're within your first couple of years of transition. Avoid getting involved with newly separated or newly divorced people. They have a lot of healing to go through before they are ready for a healthy relationship. They will be a different person a year or two from now. It takes time to get your head on straight. Be patient. Keep working on yourself. Your willingness to read this far into this book shows you believe in yourself enough to work toward healing.

7. Healthy boundaries are for your protection. It's not that you're shutting out someone. Boundaries guard you, and they reflect the respect you have for yourself. As time went on after my divorce I learned to honor myself by having and defining limits and conditions. I learned to avoid getting involved too quickly. As a girlfriend so eloquently stated, "He wanted wonderful sex, while I thought he wanted wonderful me." Boundaries are important. If you are worth it, he or she will wait for you and will treat you well. If not, you are worth more than he or she deserves. Trust God in this!

8. Your first relationship may be an attempt to escape your pain. What I call the healing relationship is an attempt to fill the void and escape the pain in your life through someone else. Guard yourself (and the other person) by being as honest as you can about what the relationship is or is not. Write out your own description of the relationship. Does it look healthy on paper?

9. Some of us are attracted to strong people so we don't have to be strong. This is true of both men and women. I have met some

wonderful men who loved being with strong women. Eventually I realized some of them were drawn to strong women because they preferred not to be strong themselves. I didn't want to be strong for anyone else. Strength should be shared between two adults. Without mutual respect, in time you will dislike and ultimately despise this person. This may sound harsh, but it's better to recognize it now so you can make good choices in your relationships. Don't be the rescuer for the sake of having a relationship.

10. Handling disagreements constructively and respectfully is critical in a relationship. If you cannot argue well, you cannot live together well, and the relationship will have a hard time surviving. Listening conveys respect. It allows each of you to explain your viewpoint and honor your right to have one. Acknowledge what the other person says. Empathize with what your partner is saying. Instead of being defensive, be curious about the other person's views. Conflict is an opportunity to deepen a relationship if it is healthy.

11. You may go through some "experimental" relationships while dating. You may find yourself exploring new worlds, having different adventures, and trekking through unfamiliar territory. Experimental relationships are with people who totally contrast who you are and what your past life has held. They may be okay to visit, but consider whether you could introduce these people to your kids, have them over for Thanksgiving, or live their lifestyle over time. The wrong relationship helps clarify what the right one is.

12. When it's over, it's over. Be aware that in every relationship you are connecting with people who have the potential to be hurt. Sometimes the kindest thing you can do is to break off a relationship when you know it's not leading anywhere, especially if the other

party wants it to become long term and you don't. Let them go find someone who will love them in the way they want and need to be loved.

FOUR SEASONS

We can't know someone until we've seen them through a *minimum* of four seasons. In a year's time you will find out what happens when they get mad, how they handle emergencies, how they value and treat their family members, and even how they handle the servers in a restuarant. You will observe family traditions and how they react when the vending machine eats their quarters or the stock market devalues their investments. Core values emerge during a year's time if you're observant enough to notice them.

Like a racecar driver, if you ignore red flags you put your life at risk. Be honest with yourself about the truth of your relationships. The issues that surface won't go away. I know, because I've tried to ignore them. Those issues you rationalized away will resurface after you've truly opened your heart and made yourself vulnerable. Face them now, because denying their existence postpones and magnifies the problem to address at a later date. It's hard to be so brutally honest when you desperately want things to work. But for your heart's long-term salvation and your own well-being, pay close attention to those red flags so you can move toward a healthy relationship. The man who has a heart for children will not have a healthy relationship dating a woman who has no desire to be with or have children. Ignoring this difference will only cause pain in the future. Listen to your heart, your gut, God, and know when to move on.

CLARIFYING QUESTIONS ON DATING

To find the perfect person is impossible because no one is perfect. But there are a few questions that can help clarify what's perfect for you if you are considering dating.

- Does this person honor me in our relationship? How do they show it?
- Does the person ask my opinion and respect my input?
- Would this person be there for me if I lost the capacity to function in areas such as health, finances, or emotions?
- Would this person prioritize me over their friends?
- Does this person love my children?
- Does this person also value my body in a non-sexual way, wanting me to be healthy and safe?
- How does this person handle my sensitivities and what is important to me?
- How does this person value the opposite sex in relationships (mother, father, daughter, son, etc.)?

Look for the perfect person for you. Set your standards high. If this forces you to be alone for a longer period, at least you'll be alone with dignity and inner peace.

The heart has its reasons that reason knows not of.

Blaise Pascal

ADVENTURES OF THE HEART

Love and relationships will never be an exact science. They profoundly affect our lives, and the more we seek to understand ourselves and what we need, the more we are able to recognize it when it comes.

Throughout my dating experience, I've experienced adventures I would never have had on my own. I've been proposed to, let down lightly, and given opportunities to know when it was time to leave. I got to know men who showed me the world and introduced me to cultures, languages, and brilliant conversations. I encountered men who were gorgeous on the outside, men who were gorgeous on the inside, men with issues, men who told fanciful stories, and men who created instant attraction but lacked substance. I met those who showed me their hearts and those who never could, men who only wanted to play, and men who had forgotten how to play.

I got to know men who were still searching for themselves and their dreams, even though their hair was turning gray. And I found men who will always be my dear friends. I can't imagine my life without them. But what they all taught me, most of all, is that I must make my own life, find my own peace, and create my own happiness.

I don't know where you come from or what scars or fears you carry from past relationships, but in your dating adventures you'll meet those who will think you are the most wonderful person in the world. Others won't give you a second chance. Be open to the possibilities and seek opportunities to meet new people. Your presence will add to their lives as well. They will intrigue you, fascinate you, and at times frustrate you. Some of the people you meet will treat you like royalty, and others, like a pauper. Maybe you'll try the paragraph test or the breakfast table test as you attempt to uncover the truth of your relationship. You'll need to be strong enough to face that truth when it comes. And if you don't get what you want, being single will work out beautifully. The greatest relationship is first with God and then with yourself.

10

START YOUR NEW LIFE NOW

I wanted a perfect ending. Now I've learned, the hard way, that some poems don't rhyme, and some stories don't have a clear beginning, middle, and end. Life is about not knowing, having to change, taking the moment and making the best of it, without knowing what's going to happen next. Delicious ambiguity.

Gilda Radner

Consider how far you've come since you first learned you were facing a divorce. The persistence and determination that brought you to this book's final chapter will propel you into the rest of your life story. You can live this new life, and you can live it well. Many people blossom after this major life event. You can choose to stay stuck or to launch, rocketing into your future, which is still unwritten. Declare, on the rooftop or within your determined heart, "The next chapter of my story will be powerful. God's got this." You can surprise yourself, emerge stronger than you ever thought possible, and live a life more meaningful and wonderful than you ever dreamed existed.

With each new day, the intensity of your past crisis will fade. You are bigger than this crisis, and you rose to face the challenges, one day and one decision at a time. While the past has hurt you, it did not defeat you. Divorce does not define who you are. This is your powerful and individual choice.

LIVING ALL THE DAYS OF YOUR LIFE

Perspective is everything. Life is not what happens to you; it's how you react to its events and your courage to move forward that makes all the difference. I hope you now have some clarity on the direction you want your life to go in. I hope you have written out your dreams and new goals (or old ones rediscovered) and with bold prayers you take action to make them come true. You have to be the one to redesign your life. If you make this transition with determination and focus, you will find the list of what is really important is very short, and your definition of success becomes simple, authentic, and undiluted.

You may find the definition of success is not elusive at all but is found within the very basics of life. I did. For me, success is found in my relationship with God, my ministry for God, and my wonderful children and grandchildren I love so much. Undoubtedly, you will discover who your true family is and who your real friends are through this transition. You will see who sticks by you through your toughest times. You will never forget their kindness, and you will cherish them for a lifetime.

Through this process, you will discover that no man or woman is an island. You and I need other people in our lives, and we need to contribute to the lives of others to give our life meaning. Start pursuing authentic friendships that provide a heart-to-heart relationship and go beyond superficial levels. Do not withdraw and isolate yourself right now. Be proactive in creating your network of friends. Ask people out for coffee or lunch. Seek out those who are emotionally healthy and provide positive reinforcement for who you want to become.

In my ReBuilding Your Life after Divorce class we talk a lot about the importance of risk. Nothing happens without it. I cannot emphasize this enough, especially now. If you truly want to live your life, you must take smart risks. Within those risks you will find your brilliance and discover your potential.

Redefining your life takes honesty and courage to shift a paradigm that has been true for so many years. Embrace a new perspective that you can be strong and whole, and act on it. To succeed in singleness is to see it as an opportunity for wonderful personal change. It is a transition within the heart.

It might not be done flawlessly, but with God's grace we get through. Harrison Salisbury states so beautifully, "There is no shortcut to life. To the end of our days, life is a lesson imperfectly learned."[1] Make your intentions pure, and the best will follow.

PIVOTAL ACTIONS TO MAKE A NEW LIFE

If you could take just three pivotal actions from this book to assist you in the transition into a new life, I would encourage you to …

Strengthen God's presence to remain grounded.

Choose to remain grounded in God's presence. Find Him in prayer and in your daily world working in your faith and giving you favor. Seek Him with your whole heart, attend church, listen to biblical teachings, learn about Him. The Scriptures are solid and foundational to life. Their principles will never change, and they can help you level out the roller coaster of emotions. They will underscore your value, regardless of what any former spouse may have said. I was amazed how personal God became to me during this time. I read the Bible again, this time desperately and personally opening myself up to it.

Be conscious of the quality of your decisions.

Make wise decisions during this critical time of transition. Your decisions will affect the rest of your life. Establish your network and tap into the wisdom of others. My choice to leave the big house in the country, though difficult, was a wise decision. By making solid decisions you will overcome your newly found insecurities and become more confident in those decisions. Pay attention to the "big picture" of your future. Your decisions impact those around you, especially your children. Your choices can make or break your relationship with them and influence their level of respect for you for the rest of their lives. This is a powerful and fragile time. Make sure you're ready to live with the results of your choices for a very long time if not for the rest of your life.

Be open and willing to take intelligent risks.

Calculated risks force us to grow and become more confident. To risk is to step out, have faith in yourself, have faith in God, and believe He will see you through in your future. If you wish to create the rest of your beautiful story, you must try new ideas and possibilities. Every success in life requires risks of some sort. Elbert Hubbard said it well: "The greatest mistake you can make in life is to be continually fearing you will make one."[2]

Be willing to stretch yourself, and don't always be predictable. Evaluate your options and take action. Again, this will involve taking risks. If you don't succeed the first time, claim the lesson and learn from it. Be kind to yourself and smile at your mistakes. It means you're human like the rest of us. Don't let past mistakes keep you from trying something new. When you step outside your comfort zone, congratulate yourself for your willingness to try. Take life beyond your present world into greater experiences and deeper knowledge.

Risk by opening yourself up to new things. Look up, look out, and expand your world. There is too much to do, too many places to explore, and too many fascinating people to meet for you to stay hidden. In your current life, you have people who care about you, love you, and want you to succeed. You'll meet new people in the future who will do the same. Someone in the world is waiting to meet you, and they need you in their life as much as you need them in yours. Live life beyond the everyday routines, and take heart in all you see before you.

A broken heart is a tender teacher, and divorce is as painful as it is powerful. Cherish the preciousness of love and the fragility of life—embrace your lessons by living life fully and not wasting any days.

SINGLE THOUGHTS

- What actions do you need to take now to start your new life? Write at least three actions that will launch you on the journey of your new life.
- How might those actions influence and change your future?
- How will you hold yourself accountable to celebrate something each day?

CREATE YOUR NEW LIFE OF PASSION

The American Heritage dictionary defines *passion* as "boundless enthusiasm, the object of such love or desire; an abandoned display of emotions."[3] To be passionate means to be capable of experiencing powerful positive emotions. Connect with your passion. Find that love and inner drive, and rekindle the things that excite you, the things you may have forgotten with the stresses of life. Where is your passion? Uncover it, explore it, and start living it. Rediscover your favorite hobbies, intellectual pursuits, outdoor activities, or other creative quests. Get your juices flowing. Whatever you pursue, recognize that passion enriches your life. Connect your passions to the dreams of your future and how you want your life to be. Awaken your curiosity. Your life was never meant to be ordinary. It is meant to be lived passionately. Rediscover passion for your own pursuits and God's plans.

THE UPSIDE OF BEING SINGLE

There are many good sides to being single. You can take on the world and make it your own. I have discovered one great part of being single is the freedom I enjoy, the tighter control I have over my own life, and the uninhibited opportunity to create and write and serve God through serving people. Now is your time to find joy in being single. Marvel at the new dynamics in your life, full of opportunity to renew who you are. Notice the changes that can be exciting for you; choose the perspective of gratitude and look at the things that are full in your life rather than the things you feel are missing.

For the suddenly single, accountability takes on a whole new meaning:

- You are accountable to God, to your conscience, and to your family in a whole new way.
- You can control your finances, adding freedom and power to your life. Being fiscally responsible gives you confidence in the present and for your future.
- You can create your own peace; the turmoil of the past and this transition is over. You have more control over your life than you ever had before. No one is disapproving or tying up your time and energy. Peace is priceless.

- You determine where you will devote your time. For example, you will have more time to spend in creative ways, such as volunteering for a good cause. What is your favorite charity? The women's shelter, your church, the PTO, a fund-raiser for a park project? What about a mission trip? Seek fulfillment in serving other people's needs. It will refresh you and fill your life with wonderful things, including the fulfillment you may be searching for. Refresh yourself by refreshing others and by helping them find their dreams.

- You have time to pursue your own interests: theater, pottery class, book club, soccer, night courses, writing, painting, or touring. You'll discover time to play, stay out late, or go to concerts (the ones you missed in high school or college). Try the opera for the first time. How about breakfast at midnight with a friend? This could be a liberating time for you. And being single could lessen the obligation of cooking balanced meals. Will the kids mind if you have peanut butter and jelly or cereal for dinner once in a while? Keep it balanced but make it simple. What's the good part of the new household now? Paint the walls purple or mount motorcycle parts to your walls—or mount purple motorcycle parts on your purple walls. Get creative with cooking, exactly how you want it. Make it as extravagant or as simple as you wish. Where is that recipe book? You can make larger portions and invite a friend to share it with you. Food is the great socializer.

- Housework can be changed with new duties and new delegations. Be creative. You can decide to take a morning run or clean the house that morning. Change the routines to suit you and your household. Embrace the peace and the freedom to redesign your life inside and out. You have a new slate and a new start.

- Make new traditions for the holidays. Keep the favorite ones of the past, but create fresh traditions to mark your new life. It will allow you to find hope through the holidays of transition, and new traditions offer more reasons to celebrate. Your first holidays will probably require a time to mourn, so give yourself the time and then move on to creating your new holiday.

REACH IN, REACH OUT

Compensate for not having a "relationship" by having many relationships. Create your network by initiating a day out with friends. Don't wait to be asked; make the first move. Ask someone to join you for a movie and dinner. Surprise someone with a favor. Buy chocolate for your department at work. Nurture friendships by being a good friend. Send a card or make a homemade gift.

Bless yourself by giving to others and delighting in their reactions. Cultivate relationships that are a positive influence in your life, ones that build you up and encourage you. As you heal and become more complete, you will find you don't have the energy for unhealthy relationships. Set boundaries, so you can let go of the people who aren't good for you. Love them from a distance but release them. Find positive, intelligent people to hang out with. Become the person others want to be around. Redefine your relationships, deepen your connections, and create a new, authentic deep bond with those you care about.

Maybe your path will never include the man or woman of your dreams. That does not mean life won't be wonderful and full of incredible adventures. Go and live your life in extraordinary style as a single. Your world is full of possibilities, and there is no way to predict the future. Live your life as a whole person. Live life on purpose and live it lightly, not taking things too seriously or sweating the minutiae, which only bogs you down. Find some fun friends to keep you vibrant and alive. Learn from their interesting perspectives and insights. Rediscover the joy of laughter and remind yourself to laugh. Make a sign and hang it in your kitchen if you must, but find the time to laugh. Be open to the new, the different, and the intriguing. Rediscover the eccentric and those who have extreme views. They will either validate your own views or open you up to new ones. Now, go back and reread this chapter and highlight those suggestions you are willing to start now.

SINGLE-MINDEDNESS

Where do you go from here? Will you empower yourself to live a successful life? The right idea at the right time can inspire you to act. This book's purpose is to inspire you to act, to move you into your greatest adventure, your greatest life. And it begins now.

Divorce is a strange way to get you where you are now, but this is where you are. Accept what is, accept where you are, and make it beautiful. Go after your own life with all the enthusiasm it deserves. The future is there for you to approach, to confront, and to experience. If you stop to truly think about it, more choices stand before you now than ever before. No one owes you a living, but you owe yourself a life. By taking some practical approaches to this new single life, it can be a wonderful one. I know; I've lived it. You can find joy again. You can smile, laugh, cherish, and love those who are dear to you. Who knows, after a time of healing you may even fall in love again. But don't wait for it; start your life now. As you begin this powerful time in making your new life, accept the new challenges along with the gift of every moment. By finding yourself suddenly single, you may just discover you are suddenly loving it!

ACKNOWLEDGMENTS

Alice Crider and Margot Starbuck, my editors—There are many stories in every writer that would never be shared without the brilliance of the editor. I am forever grateful.

Phil Mitchell, my financial expert—Thank you for being trustworthy.

Beth Bolthouse, a spiritual and psychological adviser—Thank you for your love for God and your love for the grieving. I see you carry their pain and hold them while they grieve. You are my godly example.

The group members, the hundreds of people whom I've had the privilege to walk with on their journey through divorce and redesigning their lives—Your wide eyes so full of fear became eyes of hopefulness, determination, and beautiful purpose. You inspire me. God always shows up in our groups, like He does in our lives when we ask Him.

The many churches who have allowed me to minister through Divorce Support Anonymous programs and ReDesigning Your Life (the information now found in *Suddenly Single Workbook: Building Your Future after Divorce*)—My prayer is that these programs have been the true church, meeting people in their deepest and most vulnerable need, providing the hope of Christ, the compassion of Christ, and the direction of Christ.

Todd Neimeyer—For your vision to take this message global. God used you, and I am grateful.

SINGLE VERSES TO LIVE BY

FEARS

For God has not given us a spirit of fear, but of power and of love and of a sound mind.

—2 Timothy 1:7 NKJV

So do not fear, for I am with you; do not be dismayed, for I am your God. I will strengthen you and help you; I will uphold you with my righteous hand.

—Isaiah 41:10

Do not be anxious about anything, but in every situation, by prayer and petition, with thanksgiving, present your requests to God. And the peace of God, which transcends all understanding, will guard your hearts and your minds in Christ Jesus.

—Philippians 4:6–7

For I am the LORD your God who takes hold of your right hand and says to you, Do not fear; I will help you.

—Isaiah 41:13

The Spirit you received does not make you slaves, so that you live in fear again; rather, the Spirit you received brought about your adoption to sonship. And by him we cry, "*Abba*, Father."

—Romans 8:15

But even if you should suffer for what is right, you are blessed. "Do not fear their threats; do not be frightened."

—1 Peter 3:14

There is no fear in love. But perfect love drives out fear, because fear has to do with punishment. The one who fears is not made perfect in love.

—1 John 4:18

Have I not commanded you? Be strong and courageous. Do not be afraid; do not be discouraged, for the LORD your God will be with you wherever you go.

—Joshua 1:9

GETTING CLEAR

Wait for the LORD; be strong and take heart and wait for the LORD.

—Psalm 27:14

If any of you lacks wisdom, you should ask God, who gives generously to all without finding fault, and it will be given to you.

—James 1:5

Trust in the LORD with all your heart and lean not on your own understanding; in all your ways submit to him and he will make your paths straight.

—Proverbs 3:5–6

DEFINING YOUR SUCCESS

What good is it for someone to gain the whole world, yet forfeit their soul?

—Mark 8:36

Keep this Book of the Law always on your lips; meditate on it day and night, so that you may be careful to do everything written in it. Then you will be prosperous and successful.

—Joshua 1:8

He holds success in store for the upright, he is a shield to those whose walk is blameless.

—Proverbs 2:7

YOUR FUTURE

"For I know the plans I have for you," declares the LORD, "plans to prosper you and not to harm you, plans to give you hope and a future."

—Jeremiah 29:11

Peace I leave with you; my peace I give you. I do not give to you as the world gives. Do not let your hearts be troubled and do not be afraid.

—John 14:27

Hold firmly to the word of life. And then I will be able to boast on the day of Christ that I did not run or labor in vain.

—Philippians 2:16

There is surely a future hope for you, and your hope will not be cut off.

—Proverbs 23:18

You are the light of the world. A town built on a hill cannot be hidden. Neither do people light a lamp and put it under a bowl. Instead they put it on its stand, and it gives light to everyone in the house. In the same way, let your light shine before others, that they may see your good deeds and glorify your Father in heaven.

—Matthew 5:14–17

BREAKING THE BLOCKS

I keep my eyes always on the LORD. With him at my right hand, I will not be shaken.

—Psalm 16:8

You will keep in perfect peace those whose minds are steadfast, because they trust in you.

—Isaiah 26:3

I have told you these things, so that in me you may have peace. In this world you will have trouble. But take heart! I have overcome the world.

—John 16:33

The LORD your God is in your midst, a victorious warrior. He will exult over you with joy, He will be quiet in His love, He will rejoice over you with shouts of joy.

—Zephaniah 3:17 NASB

Wisdom shouts in the street, she lifts her voice in the square.... "Turn to my reproof, behold I will pour out my spirit on you; I will make my words known to you."

—Proverbs 1:20, 23 NASB

Your ears will hear a word behind you: "This is the way, walk in it," whenever you turn to the right or to the left.

—Isaiah 30:21 NASB

When hard pressed, I cried to the LORD; he brought me into a spacious place. The LORD is with me; I will not be afraid. What can mere mortals do to me?

—Psalm 118:5–6

When anxiety was great within me, your consolation brought me joy.

—Psalm 94:19

POWER

Wisdom makes one wise man more powerful than ten rulers in a city.

—Ecclesiastes 7:19

I am not ashamed of the gospel, because it is the power of God that brings salvation to everyone who believes: first to the Jew, then to the Gentile.

—Romans 1:16

For the message of the cross is foolishness to those who are perishing, but to us who are being saved it is the power of God.

—1 Corinthians 1:18

To one there is given through the Spirit ... another miraculous powers, to another prophecy, to another distinguishing between spirits, to another speaking in different kinds of tongues, and to still another the interpretation of tongues.

—1 Corinthians 12:8, 10

I pray that out of his glorious riches he may strengthen you with power through his Spirit in your inner being.

—Ephesians 3:16

I pray that you ... may have power, together with all the saints, to grasp how wide and long and high and deep is the love of Christ.

—Ephesians 3:17–18

Finally, be strong in the Lord and in his mighty power.

—Ephesians 6:10

Therefore confess your sins to each other and pray for each other so that you may be healed. The prayer of a righteous person is powerful and effective.

—James 5:16

In a loud voice they were saying: "Worthy is the Lamb, who was slain, to receive power and wealth and wisdom and strength and honor and glory and praise!"

—Revelation 5:12

NOTES

CHAPTER 2

1. "Christine Mason Miller," Goodreads.com, accessed August 7, 2017, www.goodreads.com/quotes/search?utf8=✓&q=christine+mason +miller&commit=Search.

CHAPTER 3

1. Debbie McDaniel, "40 Powerful Quotes from Corrie ten Boom," Crosswalk. com, last modified May 21, 2015, www.crosswalk.com/faith/spiritual-life /inspiring-quotes/40-powerful-quotes-from-corrie-ten-boom.html.

2. Corrie ten Boom, *The Hiding Place* (New York: Bantam Books, 1974), 26.

3. Ron Nydam, "Forgiveness" (lecture, Calvin College, Grand Rapids, MI, 2004).

CHAPTER 4

1. "Charles Caleb Colson Quotes," BrainyQuote.com, accessed August 8, 2017, www.brainyquote.com/quotes/quotes/c/charlescal101744.html.

CHAPTER 5

1. Roger Fisher and William L. Ury, *Getting to Yes: Negotiating Agreement without Giving In* (New York: Penguin, 2011).

CHAPTER 6

1. Kerry Close, "The Average U.S. Household Owes More than $16,000 in Credit Card Debt," *Time*, December 20, 2016, http://time.com/money/4607838/household-credit-card-debt/.

2. "Eight Things a Credit Card User Should Know," *Frontline*, PBS.org, November 23, 2004, www.pbs.org/wgbh/pages/frontline/shows/credit/eight/.

3. Penny Rosema, email message to author, January 2017.

4. Neal Gabler, "The Secret Shame of Middle Class Americans," *The Atlantic* 317, no. 4 (May 2016): 52.

5. Benjamin Franklin, *Autobiography of Benjamin Franklin* (New York: MacMillian, 1901), 183.

6. "Abigail Van Buren Quotes," AZQuotes.com, accessed August 7, 2017, www.azquotes.com/quote/519340.

CHAPTER 7

1. "Unmarried and Single Americans Week: September 18–24, 2016," US Census Bureau, last updated August 26, 2016, www.census.gov/content/dam/Census/newsroom/facts-for-features/2016/CB16-FF.18.pdf.

2. Bill Hybels, "Five Critical Questions" (lecture, The Global Leadership Summit, South Barrington, IL, August 8–9, 2013), accessed October 26, 2017, www.willowcreek.com/events/leadership/docs/BH_5CriticalQuestions_Guidelines.pdf.

3. E. E. Cummings, Goodreads.com, accessed August 28, 2017, www.goodreads.com/quotes/4889-to-be-nobody-but-yourself-in-a-world-which-is.

CHAPTER 8

1. Dean Ornish, *Love and Survival* (New York: HarperCollins, 1998), 39.

2. Jane Helmstead, email message to author, August 2017.

3. Beth Bolthouse, email message to author, February 19, 2017.

CHAPTER 9

1. Georgia Shaffer, LinkedIn message to author, August 24, 2017.

CHAPTER 10

1. Harrison Salisbury, quoted in *Touchstones: A Book of Daily Meditations for Men* (Center City, MN: Hazelden, 1991), 138.

2. Elbert Hubbard, *A Thousand & One Epigrams Selected from the Writings of Elbert Hubbard* (East Aurora, NY: The Roycrofters, 1911), 77.

3. *American Heritage Dictionary*, 5th ed., s.v. "passion."

More **SUDDENLY SINGLE** resources

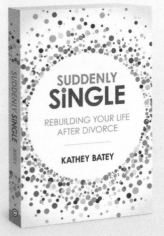

SUDDENLY SINGLE
A Compassionate Guide through the Challenges of Divorce

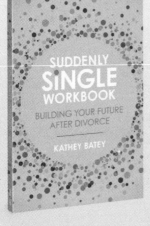

SUDDENLY SINGLE WORKBOOK
An Eight-Week Journey into Your New Life Story

SUDDENLY SINGLE JOURNAL
A Place to Process, Plan, and Dream Again

Available wherever books are sold

DAVID C COOK

transforming lives together